A Collection of Sweets, Treats, & Female Feats

Karen Cuneo & Grace Cuneo Lineman

Empowdered Sugar

Turner Publishing Company

Nashville, Tennessee

www.turnerpublishing.com

Cover design: Allison Murray

Illustrations: Allison Murray

Book design: Stacy Wakefield Forte

Library of Congress Cataloging-in-Publication Data

Names: Cuneo, Karen, author. | Cuneo-Lineman, Grace, author.
Title: Empowered sugar : a collection of sweets, treats, and female feats
  / Karen Cuneo and Grace Cuneo Lineman.
Description: Nashville : Turner Publishing Company, [2019]
Identifiers: LCCN 2019006648 (print) | LCCN 2019980230 (ebook) | ISBN
  9781684423095 (pbk.) | ISBN 9781684423101 (hardcover) | ISBN
  9781684423118 (ebook)
Subjects: LCSH: Desserts. | Baking. | International cooking. | Gifted
  women. | LCGFT: Cookbooks.
Classification: LCC TX773 .C83 2019 (print) | LCC TX773 (ebook) | DDC
  641.86--dc23
LC record available at https://lccn.loc.gov/2019006648
LC ebook record available at https://lccn.loc.gov/2019980230

9781684423095 Paperback
9781684423101 Hardcover
9781684423118 Ebook

Printed in the United States of America

17 18 19 20 10 9 8 7 6 5 4 3 2 1

Dedication:

To our Mom and Dad—
Thanks for giving me my sister.

Table of Contents

"I suppose I could have stayed home and baked cookies and had teas, but what I decided to do was to fulfill my profession."

—Hillary Clinton, 1992

Our Story

There is something delightfully ironic about a cookbook inspired by female empowerment. Baking is hardly the emblem of women's liberation. Indeed, the very goal of the women's liberation movement was to demand more space for women outside the kitchen. The chauvinistic idea that women belong in the

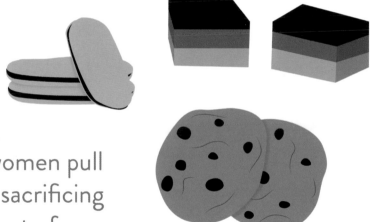

kitchen has made many women pull in the opposite direction, sacrificing the pride and empowerment of baking in the process. But for us, baking has always been equal parts art and science, and simply badass. We want to take back baking one cookie at a time.

We were first introduced to the joy of baking through the literary work of none other than Laura Ingalls Wilder. Almost every night before we went to bed, our mother read *Little House in the Big Woods* or *Little House on the Prairie* to us. We were in awe after hearing the affection with which Wilder described the brown sugar and brown syrup cakes of her own childhood, and our mother let each of us try a teaspoon of brown sugar for the first time. It was such a special moment. We felt like we now understood Wilder, her words jumping off the page. Every time we look at crystal-textured brown sugar, a tinge of nostalgia brings us back to our shared bedroom, our mother bookended by our twin beds, reading to us until lights out.

Our love affair with baking continued to be inspired by smart women. Some of our fondest memories were built spending time in the kitchen after school licking batter off a spoon while the Dixie Chicks played in the background. We were in high school when we first saw Adrienne Shelley's *Waitress*, and we both read Nora Ephron's *Heartburn* in our postcollege years. Shelley and Ephron, both brilliant and witty, complemented their stories with recipes crafted by their complicated heroines, who used baking as a means to escape, empower, and persevere. We have never associated baking with submission, but rather with inspiring women who artfully executed recipes with pride.

Karen turned her love of recipe crafting into a profession, studying food science in college and entering the workforce as a food scientist. She became more adventurous and confident in the kitchen with classes like Culinary Fundamentals and Baking Science under her belt. Karen had a particular passion for creating sweet treats like cookies and pies, and Grace had a particular passion for tasting these creations. It was Karen's professional background that allowed us to bring our punny idea to life.

Empowdered Sugar first started with the Beyhive Honey Cake, a simple recipe created to celebrate Beyoncé, whom we've seen dominate the stage as the word *feminist* was emblazoned in the background. The recipe ideas—thoughtful and playful—continued from there. And as we developed the punny recipes, we began to research these heroines and realized we wanted to make this more than just a collection of recipes—we wanted it to be an opportunity to share their stories.

We were inspired by women from many different backgrounds, cultures, and careers. We were inspired by athletes, like Serena and Venus and Misty and Kerri, who form a sisterhood on the court. We were inspired by bold politicians, like Hillary Clinton, who continue to lead the fight for women's rights. We were inspired by artists, like Madonna, who encourage women to embrace their individuality. We were inspired by the women who have, through their incredible achievements, created opportunities for women far beyond the kitchen.

The idea of a cookbook filled with recipes inspired by ambitious women did not feel revolutionary to us, but rather familiar. Growing up, we were lucky to be surrounded by smart, fierce women who encouraged us to dream big. We feel proud to be a part of a time in history when more women than ever are being recognized for their successes and realize that this is only possible because of the brave commitment of the women honored throughout this book. We want the kitchen to become a place of empowerment and a source of inspiration, as it was for us, by filling it with stories of women's sweet success, because the stories of inspiring women should be as familiar as an old family recipe.

Baking Ingredients & Tools

We have aimed to create a simple, easy-to-follow cookbook filled with familiar, delicious desserts, all made with common ingredients and tools. It is all butter, all sugar, and all "treat yourself."

The recipes are written as if we are sharing them with friends because, in the end, we are. Every recipe in this book has been tested by our loving, female family members and friends. And although the recipes range from the very easy (hello, date-and-nut balls!) to the more difficult (we're looking at you, éclairs), there is nothing in here that even a novice baker cannot do. We promise.

Below is an overview of some ingredients and tools used throughout the book. However, there is one piece of advice that transcends this list: It is the importance of *mise en place*, meaning "everything in its place." Read the recipe first to ensure you have all of the ingredients and tools on hand and have the time to perform the recipe before getting started. There is no worse time to find out you only have one egg left than halfway into making a four-egg flan.

INGREDIENTS

Agave A liquid sweetener extracted from the agave plant. Agave has a neutral, sweet flavor and a thin, liquid consistency. It is a good vegan alternative to honey.

Butter When baking, always use unsalted butter. Salt will be added to the recipe separately. However, if you only have salted butter on hand, reduce the added salt by ¼ teaspoon for every ½ cup of butter.

Chocolate The authors' favorite ingredient. There are two types of chocolate, standard and melting. Once standard chocolate melts it never fully hardens again. Melting chocolate has a higher fat content and will harden again after it is melted. That is why melting chocolate is used when a coating or shell-type layer is needed. You can substitute standard chocolate for melting choclate by adding a solid fat, like coconut oil. Whether working with standard or melting chocolate, it is important to melt gently, as it can burn very quickly. You will know you went too far with chocolate when the texture changes from smooth and shiny to dull and clumpy.

Coconut Oil There are two different coconut oils used in this book—refined and unrefined. The oils are processed differently, which impacts the coconut flavor. Unrefined coconut oil will provide a stronger coconut flavor, whereas refined is a more neutral oil. They can be used interchangeably, but will impart a different taste on the final product.

Cornstarch Cornstarch absorbs and binds moisture and makes for thick pastry creams and tender shortbreads. However, do not try to add cornstarch to a hot mixture or it will clump. Cornstarch is not very flavorful, but if it is used at a high enough percentage a light, sweet corn flavor can be detected.

Egg Whites We call for pasteurized egg whites in recipes where the egg whites will remain raw. This protects against the harmful bacteria that can remain on eggshells and contaminate a recipe. Pasteurized egg whites can always be replaced with separated raw egg whites. 1 egg white = 2 tablespoons pasteurized egg whites. 2 egg whites = ¼ cup pasteurized egg whites.

Flour There are different types of flour used in this cookbook. Each flour will provide a different flavor and/or texture to baked goods, therefore they are not interchangeable. If you make cookies with almond flour when the recipe calls for all-purpose, you will have a crumbled mess on your hands.

- All-Purpose Flour: Standard flour mixture that can be used to make the majority of recipes.
- Whole Wheat Flour: Produces denser baked goods with a nuttier flavor.
- Bread Flour: Provides more structure in dough and results in a chewier, slightly denser end product.
- Cake Flour: Provides less structure and will result in an end product with a finer, more delicate crumb.
- Almond Flour: A gluten-free flour that is made of ground almonds and provides a light almond flavor. It is also referred to as almond meal.

Milk When milk is referenced in a recipe, it is whole milk. Whole milk's fat content helps to bind dough and makes for a more tender and moist end product. When milk fat content does not matter, like in icings, the recipe will indicate "milk (dairy or non-dairy)." That's a green light to use your skim, soy, almond, oat, you name it.

Oats Oats have different names depending on how they are processed and how quickly they bake. As the name implies, quick oats will bake very fast, whereas old-fashioned oats will bake slowly and provide more structure and texture in a baked good. Interchanging types of oats in a recipe is not recommended as it will have an impact on bake time and texture.

Yeast Baker's yeast is a microorganism and leavening agent used in breads and other recipes. When baking with yeast a proof time is required, which is when the yeast is activated and releases carbon dioxide, which causes the dough to rise pre-bake. For a yeast dough to properly rise, it is important to cover the dough and place in a warm spot. If your house is cold, try placing the dough in a warmer spot, such as a turned-off oven or on top of your refrigerator. It is also helpful to snap a picture of your pre-proofed dough to compare post-proof, because an hour is a long time to hold a mental image.

TOOLS

Baking Pans Baking pans come in a variety of shapes and sizes and are designated by their dimensions or volume. In this book we will always refer to the dimensions, which are typically etched on the bottom of a pan or can be measured from inner edge to inner edge. If substituting one size for another, the baking time will need to be adjusted. For example, using a smaller baking pan will make for a deeper, or thicker, baked good and will require a longer bake time. Baking pans are not to be confused with baking sheets, which are flat, rectangular trays used to bake cookies or similar-type baked goods. .

Candy Thermometer A candy thermometer is used when a mixture needs to be heated to a very high temperature, for example when making marshmallows. A candy thermometer can typically read to 400°F, whereas a meat thermometer typically only goes to 240°F.

Cookie Scoop The authors' favorite baking tool. A cookie scoop, like an ice cream scoop, will give you perfectly uniform cookies and, if you are like us, will prevent you from eating the dough that gets stuck to your fingers. Use it to scoop cookie dough or to fill cupcake tins when the batter is too thick to pour.

Double Boiler A tool to gently melt ingredients, like chocolate. You can make your own by placing a heat-resistant bowl over a pot of simmering water.

Dough Hook A dough hook is used to knead bread doughs. If a recipe calls for active dry yeast, there is a good chance you will want to use the dough hook.

Dry Measuring Cup Dry and liquid measuring cups are not created equal. Use a dry measuring cup for ingredients like flour, sugars, and nuts. Dry measuring cups are also great for adding dry ingredients to liquid ingredients in parts.

Flat Paddle Mixer The flat paddle mixer attachment for an electric mixer is used to mix batters and sweet doughs, to cream butter, or to mix any heavy mixtures.

Liquid Measuring Cup Use a liquid measuring cup for water, milk, honey, and other liquid ingredients. Liquid measuring cups are also great for pouring batter into pans or cupcake wells cleanly and accurately.

Offset Spatula A long, narrow, metal spatula that is used to neatly spread frosting on cakes or cupcakes. It is also great at scooping stuck-on cakes out of a pan that you may have forgotten to grease.

Parchment Paper This paper will prevent cookies, cakes, and the like from sticking to the pan. It also makes for a fast and easy cleanup. Not to be confused with wax paper, which will melt in your oven and will make for a very long and difficult cleanup.

Rolling Pin This classic baking tool is used to evenly roll out dough. If you are a baking regular, a sturdy and comfortable rolling pin is a must. A clean wine bottle works great in a jam too. Either way, flour your rolling pin before use.

Rubber Spatula The best tool to scrape down the sides of a bowl (you probably have one more cookie with all of the dough stuck to the sides of the bowl!) and for scraping ingredients out of jars or measuring cups.

Sifter If a recipe calls for an ingredient to be sifted, yes, you should sift it. A wire mesh or hand-crank will both work the same. Sifting aerates and removes clumps from ingredients and produces fluffier cakes and smoother icings.

Stand or Hand Mixer Almost all of the recipes in this book were made using either an electric hand mixer or stand mixer. "Mix on high (or medium or low) speed" refers to the mixer settings. Although almost anything can be mixed with a strong arm and patience, when ingredients like egg whites or cream need to be whipped into stiff peaks, an electric mixer is generally required. A stand mixer has three types of attachments—a whisk, a paddle, and a dough hook—all of which are used in this book.

Tape Measure or Ruler This may seem like a strange item for a cookbook, but many recipes need to be cut or rolled out to certain dimensions. The best way to do this is to mark parchment paper with these dimensions to use as a guide.

Whisk A handheld whisk or whisk attachment for an electric mixer will be comprised of many metal or plastic loops. It is used to blend liquid ingredients, aerate flour, and whip egg whites or creams into peaks.

Wooden Spoon Use a wooden spoon to mix fragile ingredients, like fruits, nuts, or chocolate, into heavy mixtures, such as cake batters and cookie doughs. Always wash your wooden spoon by hand, as a dishwasher can warp and splinter the wood.

Zester or Grater These are used to zest citrus and grate cheese and vegetables. Always zest a fruit before juicing.

Women
of History

Women have always been instrumental in shaping history and culture, demonstrating leadership amongst men. Joan of Arc was in her teens when she changed the course of the Hundred Years' War, and Sacagawea led a unit of men across uncharted land while carrying a newborn on her back. And although their legacies are at times understated by historians, these women serve as constant symbols of courage, patriotism, and influence. Without them, wars would have been lost, allegiances forgotten, and folklore unwritten.

Artemis

*Greek goddess of
the hunt, the moon,
animals, and childbirth;
archer; daughter of Zeus*

Throughout Greek
mythology Artemis is
portrayed as a fierce
but kind warrior
and protector of
women. When King
Agamemnon offered
to sacrifice his own
daughter, Iphigenia,
to appease the Gods,
Artemis saved the girl
by replacing her with a
doe at the altar.

Artemis Olive Oil Muffins

OLIVE OIL AND THYME MUFFINS

SERVING SIZE

Makes 12 muffins

INGREDIENTS

1 cup all-purpose flour

¼ cup cornstarch

1 teaspoon salt

1 teaspoon baking powder

¾ cup olive oil

⅔ cup whole milk

2 eggs

3 tablespoons chopped fresh thyme leaves

1. Preheat oven to 350°F and line a 12-well muffin tin with cupcake liners.

2. In a large mixing bowl sift flour and cornstarch together, then whisk in salt and baking powder.

3. In a separate medium bowl, whisk together olive oil, milk, and eggs.

4. Add thyme to liquid mixture and whisk to combine.

5. Pour liquid mixture into flour mixture about ⅓ cup at a time, and whisk until combined after each addition.

6. Fill muffin wells with batter until about full and bake for 20 to 25 minutes, or until a golden crust forms on the top and a toothpick comes out clean when inserted. Allow muffins to cool partially in tray before transferring to a cooling rack to finish cooling completely.

BREADS

Betsy Ross

Credited with sewing the first American flag, American revolutionary, first female to have an automotive bridge named in her honor

Betsy Ross, a symbol of revolutionary patriotism, is credited with creating the first American flag after a rumored visit from George Washington. She is said to have influenced the design, changing the stars from a six-pointed style to the five-pointed style used today. Ross is confirmed to have sewn flags for the Pennsylvania State Navy Board.

Betsy Ross American Flag Cake

VANILLA CAKE WITH ALMOND FROSTING AND BERRIES

SERVING SIZE
Serves 12 to 18

INGREDIENTS

Cake
2½ cups all-purpose flour
½ teaspoon salt
1 cup unsalted butter, softened (2 sticks)
1½ cups granulated sugar
2½ teaspoons baking powder
1 tablespoon vanilla extract
3 eggs
1 cup whole milk
½ cup heavy cream

1   Preheat oven to 350°F and grease a 9-inch x 13-inch baking dish.

2   FOR THE CAKE: Sift flour and salt together in a medium mixing bowl and set aside.

3   In a large mixing bowl, mix butter, sugar, baking powder, and vanilla extract together with an electric mixer on high speed until fluffy, about 5 minutes.

4   Add eggs, one at a time, mixing until combined after each addition.

5   Alternate between adding dry ingredients, about ½ a cup at a time, and milk and cream. Beat until combined after each addition.

6   Pour batter into baking dish and bake for 30 to 35 minutes, or until edges start to brown and a toothpick comes out clean when inserted. Cool completely in the pan.

continued →

CAKES & CUPCAKES

Frosting

½ cup unsalted butter, softened (1 stick)

2 cups powdered sugar

1 tablespoon milk (dairy or non-dairy), plus additional as needed

¼ teaspoon vanilla extract

¼ teaspoon almond extract

½ cup blueberries

1 cup sliced strawberries

7   **FOR THE FROSTING:** While cake is cooling, beat butter with an electric mixer on high speed until fluffy.

8   Sift in powdered sugar and add milk, vanilla extract, and almond extract. Mix until combined. Add an additional 1 to 2 teaspoons milk if frosting is too thick to spread.

9   Once cake has cooled, place a serving plate on top of cake and flip over to remove cake from the dish with the domed side down.

10   Spread frosting evenly across the entire cake.

11   Arrange blueberries in lines across the top left sixth of the cake (4½-inch x 4-inch rectangle).

12   Cut strawberries into thin slices and arrange in even horizontal lines across cake, leaving a 1-inch space between each row.

Cleopatruffles

BIRTHDAY CAKE TRUFFLES

SERVING SIZE

Makes 2 to 3
dozen truffles

INGREDIENTS

Cake

2½ cups all-purpose flour

½ teaspoon salt

1 cup unsalted butter,
softened (2 sticks)

1½ cups granulated sugar

2½ teaspoons
baking powder

1 tablespoon
vanilla extract

3 eggs

1 cup whole milk

½ cup heavy cream

Frosting

½ cup unsalted butter,
softened (1 stick)

2 cups powdered sugar

1 tablespoon milk
(diary or non-dairy)

¼ teaspoon vanilla extract

½ cup rainbow sprinkles

1. Preheat oven to 350°F and grease a 9-inch x 13-inch baking dish.

2. **FOR THE CAKE:** Sift flour and salt together in a medium mixing bowl and set aside.

3. In a large mixing bowl, mix butter, sugar, baking powder, and vanilla extract together with an electric mixer on medium speed until fluffy, about 5 minutes.

4. Add eggs one at a time, mixing until incorporated after each addition.

5. Alternate between adding dry ingredients, about ½ cup at a time, and adding milk and cream. Mix until combined after each addition.

6. Pour batter into baking dish and bake for 30 to 35 minutes, or until edges start to brown and a toothpick comes out clean when inserted. Allow cake to cool completely in pan.

7. **FOR THE FROSTING:** While cake is cooling, mix butter with an electric mixer on high speed until fluffy.

8. Sift in powdered sugar and add milk and vanilla extract. Mix until combined. If frosting is too thick to mix easily by hand, add an additional teaspoon of milk. Gently fold sprinkles into frosting.

continued →

White Chocolate Coating

2 cups white chocolate chips (16 ounces)

3 tablespoons refined coconut oil

9 Once cake is cooled, crumble into a large mixing bowl and add frosting. Mix on medium speed until the cake and frosting can be formed into balls.

10 Line a baking sheet with parchment paper. Roll 1-tablespoon portions of cake mixture into truffles, place on the parchment paper, and refrigerate for 30 minutes.

11 FOR THE WHITE CHOCOLATE COATING: While truffles are cooling, melt white chocolate in a medium microwave-safe bowl by microwaving in 30-second intervals, stirring between each interval. Stir in coconut oil until smooth.

12 Once truffles are cooled, drop the truffles into the melted chocolate to coat, and scoop out with a small slotted spoon or fork.

13 Place coated truffles back on the parchment paper. Place in the refrigerator to allow chocolate to harden completely, about 15 minutes.

Cleopatra

Last pharaoh of Egypt, diplomat, naval commander, multilinguist

Very few historical accounts of Cleopatra's reign as Egyptian Pharaoh exist. Most written history about Cleopatra comes from the biographies of men, like Mark Antony and Herod the Great. For that reason, more is known about Cleopatra's relationships with men than her accomplishments as Egypt's Pharaoh and naval commander and her scholarly writings on Greek medicine.

Rosie the Riveter

Cultural icon of WWII, symbol of female strength and economic power

The "We Can Do It" image was created in 1942 by artist J. Howard Miller for a Westinghouse poster. Renamed Rosie the Riveter, the image represents the female workers of WWII, when between 1940 and 1945, the female percentage of the US workforce increased from 27 percent to nearly 37 percent. Rosie is now a cultural representation of feminism.

Rosie's Pecan Do It Pie

BOURBON PECAN PIE

SERVING SIZE

Serves 8 to 10

INGREDIENTS

1 premade pie crust or ½ recipe Pieris Apfel Crust (page 163)

1¼ cups dark brown sugar

⅔ cup corn syrup

6 tablespoons butter

1 teaspoon salt

2 cups chopped and toasted pecans

2 tablespoons bourbon

1 tablespoon vanilla extract

½ teaspoon ground cinnamon

3 eggs

½ cup whole pecans for topping, optional

1   Preheat oven to 400°F and grease a 9-inch pie pan.

2   Roll pie crust into a 10-inch circle. Lay prepared crust in the pie pan, allowing edges to overhang by ½ inch; style edges to your liking using a fork or a spoon, or by pinching dough together with your thumb and index finger.

3   Poke holes into the bottom of the pie crust, lay parchment paper over the bottom of the crust, and fill with dried beans or weights; this will stop the pie crust from rising or bubbling.

4   Bake pie crust for about 15 minutes, or until dough is set. The dough should be soft to the touch but not sticky, with golden edges.

5   Remove parchment and weights from pie crust, place pie pan on a baking sheet, and reduce your oven temperature to 350°F.

6   To make the filling, combine brown sugar, corn syrup, butter, and salt in a medium saucepan and bring to a rolling boil over medium-high heat.

7   Allow the mixture to boil vigorously for about 1 minute, while stirring constantly with a spatula or wooden spoon. This will allow for an even distribution of heat and keep the mixture from burning to the sides of the saucepan.

continued →

PIES TARTS & COBBLERS

8   Remove saucepan from the heat and gently stir in toasted pecans, bourbon, vanilla extract, and cinnamon. Set mixture aside and allow it to cool for 3 to 5 minutes.

9   Beat eggs in a small bowl gently with a fork, then whisk eggs into filling until smooth and shiny; do not mix in the eggs while mixture is too hot or the eggs will cook.

10   Pour filling into the pie crust, arrange additional whole pecans on top of the filling, if desired, and bake for 20 minutes.

11   Remove pie from the oven and cover with foil, return the pie to the oven, and bake for an additional 20 to 25 minutes, or until center is set and no longer wiggly.

12   Allow pie to cool completely before serving.

How to Toast Nuts

Pecans, and most other nuts, can be toasted by placing on a baking sheet in a 350°F oven for 5 minutes. While time is the simplest way to track the toasty-ness of the pecans, the best way is to track with your nose. As soon as the pecans become fragrant, filling your kitchen with nutty warmth, they are done and can be removed from the oven.

Eve's Sinful Apple Pie

APPLE BOURBON PIE

SERVING SIZE
Serves 8 to 10

INGREDIENTS

5 tart, crisp apples

1 tablespoon lemon juice

1 cup granulated sugar, plus more for sprinkling

1 cup brown sugar

2 premade pie crusts or 1 recipe Pieris Apfel Crust (page 163)

2 tablespoons bourbon

1 teaspoon ground cinnamon

4 tablespoons all-purpose flour, divided

½ teaspoon salt

1. Peel apples and cut into thin slices. Toss apples in lemon juice, sugar, and brown sugar. Cover and let sit for 1 hour to release juices.

2. Preheat oven to 350°F and grease a 9-inch pie pan. Roll pie crust out into a 10-inch circle. Lay prepared crust in the pie pan, allowing edges to overhang by ½ inch. Style edges to your liking using a fork or a spoon, or by pinching dough together with your thumb and index finger. Poke holes into the bottom of the crust, lay parchment paper over the bottom of the crust, and fill with dried beans or weights; this will stop the pie crust from rising or bubbling.

3. Bake pie crust for about 15 minutes, or until dough is set. The dough should be soft to the touch but not sticky, with golden edges. When crust is baked, remove parchment and weights, place pie pan on a baking sheet, and increase oven temperature to 400°F.

continued →

PIES TARTS & COBBLERS

29

4   When apples are ready, separate from juices and set apples aside. Pour juices into a medium saucepan. Add bourbon to mixture and bring to a simmer over low heat. Allow to simmer, stirring occasionally, for 10 minutes to thicken. Remove from heat and stir cinnamon and 1 tablespoon of flour into the mixture.

5   In a small mixing bowl, whisk together remaining 3 tablespoons of flour and salt. Coat apples with flour.

6   Pour apples and liquid mixture into semi-baked crust. Do not let liquid overflow; you may have some leftover liquid.

7   Roll out second pie crust to a 10-inch circle and lay on top of apples. Press edges firmly down and cut five 2-inch slits around the center of the pie in a star-like shape. Sprinkle sugar across top of pie.

8   Bake pie on baking sheet at 400°F for 20 minutes, then reduce heat to 350°F and bake for an additional 50 minutes, or until crust is baked and golden.

Which Types of Apples Are Best for Baking?

When baking with fresh apples, you want to choose apples that are tart, sweet, and firm. Pick apples that look fresh and are firm to the touch. We recommend Crispin, Honeycrisp, and Granny Smith. Try to avoid Red Delicious.

Eve

Biblical figure, mother of humanity, and first woman according to the creation myth of Abrahamic religions

Eve, as depicted in the Book of Genesis, was tempted by a serpent to eat the forbidden fruit from the tree of the knowledge of good and evil. Eve shared the fruit with her partner, Adam. This act eventually lead to the expulsion of humans from the Garden of Eden, and Eve was punished to a life of sorrow and laborious childbirth.

Joan
of Arc

Canonized saint, "Maid of Orléans," patron saint of France, military leader

Joan of Arc, inspired by a vision from God, believed she was destined to lead France to victory in the Hundred Years' War. In a private meeting with King Charles VII, she convinced him to allow her to lead the French Army to victorious battle at Orléans despite having no military training. She was just eighteen when she was captured and tried for witchcraft, leading to her eventual death.

Joan of Bark

SWEET AND SALTY TOFFEE BARK

SERVING SIZE

Makes about 3 dozen pieces

INGREDIENTS

About 24 plain graham cracker squares

1 cup unsalted butter (2 sticks)

¼ cup granulated sugar

¼ cup brown sugar

1 cup broken thin pretzels

2 cups semisweet chocolate chips (16 ounces)

¾ cup chopped walnuts,

1. Preheat oven to 350°F and line a 10-inch x 15-inch jelly roll pan or baking sheet with aluminum foil, including sides.

2. Lay graham crackers on baking sheet or jelly roll pan in a single layer that covers the entirety of the pan. Break pieces to fill as needed.

3. In a medium saucepan, melt butter over medium heat. Whisk sugar and brown sugar into melted butter and bring to a boil. Reduce heat to low and allow to continue to bubble for 4 minutes.

4. Pour butter mixture on top of graham cracker squares, cover with broken pretzel pieces, and bake for 10 minutes.

5. Remove from the oven and let sit for 1 minute. Cover with chocolate chips and let sit for an additional 2 minutes to allow chocolate to melt. Spread melted chocolate evenly across pan with a spatula or back of a spoon.

6. Top with walnut pieces and press gently into the chocolate mixture.

7. Refrigerate for 2 hours to allow the chocolate to harden, then break into small ½-inch-to-¾-inch pieces.

Mary, Queen of Scots

Queen of Scotland, queen consort of France, mother of King James VI, initiated religious tolerance in Scotland during reign

Mary was known throughout England and Scotland for her grace, beauty, and wisdom. She ascended to the throne as queen of Scotland at just six days old, but due to others' intolerance, wars, and fear, Mary spent the majority of her life imprisoned. She was eventually beheaded at the will of her own cousin, Queen Elizabeth I, before her forty-fifth birthday.

Mary, Queen of Scotchies

BUTTERSCOTCH OATMEAL COOKIES

SERVING SIZE

Makes about 2 dozen cookies

INGREDIENTS

1 cup all-purpose flour

1 teaspoon baking soda

½ teaspoon baking powder

½ teaspoon ground allspice

¼ teaspoon salt

½ cup unsalted butter, softened (1 stick)

½ cup granulated sugar

½ cup brown sugar

1 teaspoon vanilla extract

1 egg

1½ cups quick oats

2 cups butterscotch morsels (16 ounces)

1. In a medium mixing bowl, whisk flour, baking soda, baking powder, allspice, and salt together. Set aside.

2. In a large mixing bowl, mix butter, granulated sugar, and brown sugar with an electric mixer on medium speed until creamed, about 3 minutes.

3. Add vanilla extract and egg and mix until combined.

4. Slowly add flour mixture, about ⅓ a cup at a time, and mix until combined.

5. With a wooden spoon or spatula, fold in oats and mix well. Add butterscotch morsels and continue to mix with a wooden spoon or spatula until evenly distributed.

6. Refrigerate dough for 30 minutes to 1 hour.

7. Preheat oven to 350°F and line 2 to 3 baking sheets with parchment paper.

8. Drop cookies by level tablespoons onto baking sheets and bake for 12 to 15 minutes, or until edges are starting to brown and centers are set.

9. Allow cookies to cool completely on the pan.

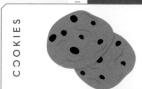

COOKIES

Nefertiti

Egyptian queen and chief consort, one of the most recognizable figures of the ancient world

The bust of Nefertiti was sculpted in ancient Egypt around 1350 BC. Discovered amongst rubble by German archaeologists in 1912, the bust has come to be recognized as an artistic symbol of female beauty and power.

Nefertitea Cookies

ORANGE TEA COOKIES

SERVING SIZE

Makes 2½ to 3 dozen cookies

INGREDIENTS

1 cup unsalted butter (2 sticks)

¾ cup powdered sugar, plus more for dusting

1 tablespoon orange zest

½ teaspoon vanilla extract

⅓ cup fresh squeezed orange juice (from about 1 large orange)

3 cups all-purpose flour

½ teaspoon salt

1. Preheat oven to 350°F and line baking sheets with parchment paper.

2. In a large mixing bowl, mix butter, powdered sugar, orange zest, and vanilla extract with an electric mixer on medium speed until creamed, about 1 to 2 minutes.

3. Add orange juice and mix until loosely combined. Some juice may still remain unincorporated.

4. Add flour and salt and mix until just combined.

5. Roll out 1-inch balls, slightly smaller than golf balls, and place on baking sheets. Bake for 15 to 20 minutes, or until bottoms start to brown and tops are set.

6. Remove from oven and allow cookies to cool completely on baking sheets. Dust with powdered sugar when cool.

COOKIES

Queen Elizabeth I

Queen of England and Ireland, monarch during England's Elizabethan era, Supreme Governor of the Church of England

Queen Elizabeth I's forty-four-year reign provided stability and identity for the English monarchy. Though some historians choose to call Elizabeth "lucky," she retained control of the throne in a time of numerous wars and governmental unrest. Elizabeth reigned over the Elizabethan Age in England, a golden age in history when literature, music, and economics thrived.

Queen Elizazested Scones

LEMON POPPY SEED SCONES

SERVING SIZE

Makes about 1½ dozen scones

INGREDIENTS

2¼ cups all-purpose flour

⅓ cup granulated sugar

1½ teaspoons baking soda

½ teaspoon cream of tartar

½ teaspoon salt

½ cup cold unsalted butter (1 stick)

1 egg

½ cup heavy cream, plus more for brushing

2 teaspoons poppy seeds

½ teaspoon vanilla extract

1½ tablespoons lemon zest

2 tablespoons lemon juice

1. Preheat oven to 375°F and line 2 large baking sheets with parchment paper.

2. In a large mixing bowl, whisk together flour, sugar, baking soda, cream of tartar, and salt.

3. Cut butter into 1-inch cubes and work into flour mixture with a wooden spoon, fork, or hands until the butter is incorporated and mixture is crumbly.

4. In a separate medium bowl, whisk egg, heavy cream, poppy seeds, and vanilla extract together. Add to flour mixture and mix with a wooden spoon or spatula until just combined.

5. Add lemon zest and lemon juice and mix until combined.

6. Transfer dough to a floured surface or floured parchment paper, divide dough into 2 equal parts, and press into 2 round disks about ½ inch thick.

7. Cut each circle into 8 triangles, like a pizza.

8. Transfer triangles to lined baking sheets and set about 2 inches apart. Brush with heavy cream for an extra golden top, if desired. Bake for 16 to 20 minutes, or until bottoms and sides just start to turn golden. Cool on baking sheets.

9. Enjoy with jam, honey, or butter, if desired.

Sacagawea

Lemhi Shoshone interpreter and guide of the Lewis and Clark expedition, honorary sergeant, inductee of the National Cowgirl Hall of Fame

Sacagawea is most famously known for her role as a guide and interpreter during the Lewis and Clark expedition. She led the discovery group along the trail by land and boat, all while caring for her newborn son. Her ability to navigate the trails by memory alone earned her the nickname "pilot," as dubbed by Clark.

Sacagawea Trail Mix Bars

WHITE CHOCOLATE TRAIL MIX BARS

SERVING SIZE

Makes about
1 dozen bars

INGREDIENTS

2 cups thin
pretzel snaps

1 cup chopped roasted
and salted cashews

½ cup unsalted
pumpkin seeds

½ cup dried cranberries

1 cup white chocolate
melting wafers
(8 ounces)

½ cup agave syrup

¼ cup refined
coconut oil

¼ cup light brown sugar

1. Line a 9-inch x 9-inch baking pan with parchment paper, including sides, and set aside.

2. In a large mixing bowl, break pretzels into 1-inch pieces.

3. Add cashews, pumpkin seeds, and cranberries to pretzels and mix until evenly distributed. Set aside.

4. In a separate bowl, melt white chocolate in a double boiler over low heat, or in the microwave at 30-second intervals, stirring between each interval. Once chocolate is melted, pour into prepared pan and spread evenly.

5. In a medium saucepan, combine agave syrup, coconut oil, and brown sugar and bring to a rolling boil over medium-high heat. Allow to remain at a rolling boil for 3 minutes, stirring occasionally.

6. Pour hot agave mixture into pretzel mixture and stir quickly with a wooden spoon or spatula to coat each piece.

7. Pour mixture over white chocolate and press down with a spatula or spoon to create an even layer. Be careful not to touch the mixture directly, as it will be very hot.

8. Allow to cool for 1 to 2 hours, or until set, before cutting into bars or square pieces.

BROWNIES
& BARS

41

Politicians
& Activists

It is because of the bravery and persistence of female politicians and activists that the voices of women, and so many other historically oppressed groups, are heard. The audacious Susan B. Anthony gave a voice to women at the polls, fearless Rosa Parks gave a voice to the civil rights movement, and Tarana Burke found a way to magnify the voices of the thousands of victims of sexual assault. Unwavering, these women have put their lives and reputations on the line to stand up for what they believe.

Susan B. Anthony

Suffragette, abolitionist, publisher, women's rights activist, founder of the National Woman Suffrage Association

"Men their rights and nothing more; women their rights and nothing less."

19th Amendmint Chocolate Chip Ice Cream

MINT CHOCOLATE CHIP ICE CREAM

SERVING SIZE

Makes 1.5 quarts

INGREDIENTS

3 egg yolks

¾ cup granulated sugar

1½ cups whole milk

¼ cup fresh mint leaves

1½ cups heavy whipping cream

2 teaspoons vanilla extract

1 tablespoon mint extract

¼ cup chopped milk chocolate (2 ounces)

1. In a saucepan off the heat, whisk egg yolks and sugar together until the sugar is fully dissolved. Set aside.

2. In a separate saucepan, heat milk over medium-low heat without stirring until the milk begins to simmer on the sides and a very thin film starts to form on the top.

3. Remove milk from heat and let cool for 30 seconds. Whisk milk slowly into egg mixture.

4. Heat mixture over medium-low heat until it reaches 165°F. Do *not* let the mixture boil.

5. Remove from heat and add fresh mint leaves. Transfer to a storage container. Place in refrigerator and let cool until the mixture reaches at least room temperature, about 5 to 6 hours.

6. When mixture is cool, remove mint leaves.

7. Whisk heavy cream, vanilla extract, and mint extract into milk-and-egg mixture and transfer to an ice cream maker. Start to churn according to the manufacturer's instructions.

8. Slowly add chocolate to ice cream maker while ice cream is churning.

9. Churn until desired texture is reached, 20 to 50 minutes, depending on the temperature of your ice cream maker. Ice cream can be served immediately or stored in an airtight container in the freezer.

Rosa Parks

Civil rights leader, Montgomery bus boycott leader, Presidential Medal of Freedom awardee, Congressional Gold Medal awardee, author

"No, the only tired I was, was tired of giving in."

Ambrosa Parks

AMBROSIA

SERVING SIZE
Serves 8 to 10

INGREDIENTS
½ cup heavy cream

½ cup full-fat plain Greek yogurt

1 tablespoon honey

1 cup canned or fresh pineapple, chopped into ½-inch pieces

¾ cup canned or frozen mandarin oranges, washed and drained

1 cup maraschino cherries, washed and drained

1 cup shredded sweetened coconut

1 cup mini marshmallows

½ cup slivered almonds, optional

1. In a large mixing bowl, whisk heavy cream with an electric mixer on medium to high speed until stiff peaks form, about 3 minutes.

2. Add Greek yogurt and honey to cream and whisk until combined.

3. Gently fold pineapples, mandarin oranges, cherries, coconut, and mini marshmallows into the whipped cream mixture.

4. Cover with plastic wrap and refrigerate for 1 hour.

5. If desired, toast slivered almonds lightly and sprinkle on top of ambrosia immediately before serving.

Fresh vs. Canned vs. Frozen

Certain recipes call for fresh, frozen, or canned fruits. Canned fruits are often packaged in sugar and water and are preferred when the juice is added for moisture or flavor. Whether to choose fresh or frozen fruits is most often a matter of convenience. For this recipe, fresh fruits can be used as long as the fruits are properly washed, peeled, and chopped.

Condoleezza Rice

First female US national security advisor, first African American female US secretary of state, professor, diplomat

"We need to move beyond the idea that girls can be leaders and create the expectation that they should be leaders."

Condoleezza Rice Pudding

RICE PUDDING

SERVING SIZE

Serves 6

INGREDIENTS

2 cups whole milk

1 cup water

½ cup long-grain white rice

⅛ teaspoon salt

1 cinnamon stick

1 egg

¼ cup light brown sugar

¼ teaspoon ground cinnamon

1 tablespoon butter

1 teaspoon vanilla extract

⅓ cup raisins, optional

1. In a medium saucepan, combine milk, water, rice, salt, and cinnamon stick. Stir well and make sure no rice is sticking to the bottom.

2. Bring mixture to a boil over high heat. Reduce the heat to low and let the mixture simmer, uncovered, for 10 minutes. Stir occasionally so that rice does not stick to the bottom of the pan.

3. Cover the mixture and allow to simmer for 15 to 20 minutes more, or until rice is completely cooked.

4. In a small mixing bowl, whisk egg and brown sugar together. Set aside.

5. Scoop ¼ cup of rice mixture out of the saucepan and allow to cool for about 2 minutes. Slowly add the cooled rice to the egg mixture while whisking constantly to temper the eggs.

6. Pour the tempered egg mixture into the remaining rice mixture in the saucepan. Stir over low heat for 5 to 10 minutes, or until mixture thickens to the desired consistency.

7. When rice reaches desired consistency, mix in cinnamon, butter, and vanilla extract and stir for 1 minute longer. Fold in raisins, if desired.

8. Remove from heat and allow pudding to cool for about 5 minutes. Enjoy hot or cold.

TRADITIONAL DESSERTS

Dolores Huerta

American labor leader, civil rights activist, co-founder of the National Farmworkers Association, Presidential Medal of Freedom awardee

"Every moment is an organizing opportunity, every person a potential activist, every minute a chance to change the world."

Dolores Huertchata

ICED HORCHATA

INGREDIENTS

¾ cup long-grain white rice

⅓ cup whole unsalted almonds

3 cinnamon sticks

3 cups warm water

¼ teaspoon vanilla extract

⅛ teaspoon salt

2 to 4 tablespoons granulated sugar or sweetener of choice

2 shots of espresso, optional

1. In a blender or food processor, blend uncooked white rice for 15 to 45 seconds. Do not pulse into a powder, only enough to break up grains slightly.

2. Transfer rice to a large airtight jar or container. Add almonds, cinnamon sticks, and warm water. Seal jar or container tightly and place in the refrigerator to steep for 8 to 12 hours.

3. Remove from refrigerator, pour into a food processor or blender, and blend until the mixture is smooth, 1 to 2 minutes.

4. Strain mixture with a nut milk bag, piece of cheesecloth, or wire mesh sieve, pressing out as much liquid as possible.

5. Stir in vanilla extract and salt, and add sugar or sweetener to taste.

6. Enjoy as is, or pour 8 ounces over ice with a shot of espresso, if desired.

Horchata will separate over time. Shake or mix well before serving.

Eleanor Roosevelt

Former First Lady of the United States, US delegate to the United Nations, human rights activist

"A woman is like a tea bag—you never know how strong she is until she gets in hot water."

Eleanor Roosevelvet Cake

RED VELVET CAKE

SERVING SIZE
Serves 10 to 12

INGREDIENTS

Cake

2½ cups all-purpose flour

¾ cup unsweetened cocoa powder

1 teaspoon baking soda

½ teaspoon salt

1 cup unsalted butter, softened (2 sticks)

2 cups granulated sugar

4 eggs

1 cup sour cream

½ cup whole milk

1½ teaspoons vanilla extract

1 tablespoon red food coloring

1. Preheat oven to 350°F. Grease two 8-inch x 2-inch round cake pans with butter or nonstick spray.

2. **FOR THE CAKE:** Sift together flour, cocoa powder, baking soda, and salt in a medium bowl.

3. In a separate large bowl, mix butter and sugar together with an electric mixer at medium speed for 5 minutes, or until light and fluffy. This will beat air into the batter and will help your cakes to rise.

4. On medium speed, mix the eggs into the mixture one at a time. Then continue to mix in sour cream, milk, vanilla extract, and red food coloring.

5. On low speed, mix in flour mixture until it is fully incorporated with no visible flour lumps.

6. Divide cake batter evenly and pour into the greased pans. Bake the cakes for 25 to 35 minutes, or until a toothpick comes out clean. Remove the cakes from the oven and set aside to cool in the pans.

continued →

CAKES & CUPCAKES

Frosting

4 cups powdered sugar

¾ cup cream cheese

½ cup butter, softened (1 stick)

1 teaspoon vanilla extract

⅛ teaspoon salt

1 to 2 teaspoons milk (dairy or non-dairy)

7   FOR THE FROSTING: While the cakes are cooling, sift powdered sugar into a medium bowl. Set aside.

8   In a separate bowl, beat cream cheese, butter, vanilla extract, and salt together with an electric mixer on a medium-high speed until fluffy, then slowly add in the powdered sugar, mixing together on low speed. If frosting is too thick to spread, add 1 to 2 teaspoons of milk.

9   When cakes are completely cool, remove from pans and set on a cooling rack or cake stand.

10 Level the top of one cake by cutting the raised rounded middle section with a serrated knife. Once leveled, add a thick layer of frosting to the top of the cake and place the remaining cake on top of the frosted layer.

11 Cover the two-tiered cake completely with the remaining frosting.

Eva Pearon Almond Tart

PEAR AND ALMOND TART

SERVING SIZE

Serves 8 to 10

INGREDIENTS

Crust

1 cup all-purpose flour

½ cup almond flour

1 tablespoon granulated sugar

¼ teaspoon salt

½ cup unsalted butter, softened (1 stick)

1 egg

1. **FOR THE CRUST:** In a large mixing bowl, whisk together all-purpose flour, almond flour, sugar, and salt.

2. Cut in butter 1 tablespoon at a time with a fork, hands, or whisk until crumbly.

3. Add egg and mix until combined and dough forms into a soft ball.

4. Transfer dough to a floured work surface or a piece of floured parchment paper. Roll out to a 10-inch disk, cover with plastic wrap, and refrigerate for 1 hour.

5. Preheat oven to 350°F and grease a 9-inch tart pan.

6. Lay crust in the tart pan, press dough firmly into edges and bottom of pan, and fold over 1-inch overhang onto edges.

7. Cover bottom of crust with parchment paper and cover parchment with baking beans, weights, or rice. Bake for 20 to 25 minutes, or until edges begin to turn golden and center is set.

continued →

Poached Pears

3 cups water

¾ cup granulated sugar

1 tablespoon lemon juice

2 whole red pears, peeled

Almond Filling

½ cup slivered almonds

½ cup granulated sugar

2 tablespoons all-purpose flour

½ teaspoon ground ginger

¼ teaspoon salt

2 tablespoons unsalted butter, softened

¼ teaspoon almond extract

1 egg

8   **FOR THE POACHED PEARS:** In a large saucepan, combine water, sugar, and lemon juice over medium-high heat and whisk until sugar is dissolved. Bring mixture to a boil. Place peeled, whole pears into water and reduce heat to a simmer. Allow pears to simmer for 20 minutes, stirring occasionally.

9   Transfer poached pears to an ice bath to stop cooking and pat dry. Core pears, cut into thin slices, and set aside.

10   **FOR THE ALMOND FILLING:** Place slivered almonds in a large mixing bowl. Mix at high speed to break up almonds slightly.

11   Add sugar, flour, ginger, salt, butter, and almond extract and mix until combined. Add egg and mix until combined.

12   Pour almond filling into tart crust and spread evenly with a spatula. Arrange pear slices on top of filling in a circle or design of choice.

13   Bake tart for 35 to 40 minutes, or until filling has puffed slightly and is set. Allow tart to cool completely and remove tart from pan before slicing.

You can use canned pear halves in place of poached pears. If using canned pear halves, skip steps 8 and 9. Cut canned pears into slices for assembly and baking.

Eva María Duarte de Perón

Former First Lady of Argentina, founder of Argentina's first large-scale female political party, women's suffrage advocate

"I demanded more rights for women because I know what women had to put up with."

Harriet Tubman

Conductor of the Underground Railroad, abolitionist, spy for the US Army, children's and women's rights activist

"I was the conductor of the Underground Railroad for eight years, and I can say what most conductors can't say; I never ran my train off the track and I never lost a passenger."

Harriet Tubman Appletionist Spiced Roll

APPLE SPICE ROLL

SERVING SIZE
Serves 10 to 12

INGREDIENTS

Cake
⅔ cup all-purpose flour

¼ cup whole wheat flour

1 teaspoon baking powder

¼ teaspoon salt

¼ teaspoon ground ginger

¼ teaspoon ground cloves

¼ teaspoon ground cinnamon

1 cup granulated sugar

3 eggs

¾ cup unsweetened applesauce

1   Preheat oven to 375°F and grease a 10-inch x 15-inch jelly roll pan, including sides.

2   **FOR THE CAKE:** In a medium mixing bowl, whisk together all-purpose flour, whole wheat flour, baking powder, salt, ginger, cloves, and cinnamon. Set aside.

3   In a large mixing bowl, mix sugar and eggs together with an electric mixer at a medium speed until foamy, about 2 minutes. Add applesauce and mix on medium speed for an additional minute.

4   Add flour mixture to wet ingredients, ⅓ of the mixture at a time, blending until combined between each addition.

5   Pour batter into greased jelly roll pan and bake for 18 to 22 minutes, or until edges begin to brown and cake is set.

6   Let cake cool for about 1 minute, then transfer to a clean kitchen towel. Starting at the short end, roll cake up tightly in the towel. Allow cake to cool in the towel completely.

continued →

CAKES & CUPCAKES

59

Frosting

3 ounces cream cheese, softened

3 tablespoons unsalted butter, softened

1½ cups powdered sugar, plus more for sprinkling, optional

¼ teaspoon ground cinnamon

¼ teaspoon vanilla extract

7   **FOR THE FROSTING:** While cake is cooling, whisk butter and cream cheese together with an electric mixer at a high speed until combined. Add powdered sugar, cinnamon, and vanilla extract and whisk on medium speed until combined and smooth.

8   Unroll cake from the towel and place on a sheet of aluminum foil. Spread the frosting evenly across the cake with a knife or offset spatula.

9   Roll the cake tightly once again and wrap in foil. Allow cake to sit for 4 to 6 hours before serving.

10   Sprinkle with powdered sugar immediately before serving, if desired.

If whole wheat flour is not already in your pantry and buying a bag to only use ¼ cup seems frivolous, you can substitute with all-purpose flour. The flavor will lose some nuttiness, but this can be offset by increasing the spices by a pinch.

I'm With Herb & Buttermilk Biscuits

HERB AND BUTTERMILK BISCUITS

SERVING SIZE

Makes 15 large or 20 small biscuits

INGREDIENTS

2½ cups all-purpose flour

1½ tablespoons baking powder

1 tablespoon granulated sugar

2 teaspoons salt

1 teaspoon black pepper

1 tablespoon fresh chopped chives, plus additional for sprinkling

10 tablespoons cold unsalted butter, plus 2 tablespoons butter, melted

1 cup buttermilk, plus additional as needed

1. Preheat oven to 425°F and grease a baking sheet with butter or non-stick spray.

2. Whisk flour, baking powder, sugar, salt, pepper, and chives together in a large mixing bowl.

3. Cut cold butter into ½-inch cubes and incorporate into the flour mixture with a fork, pastry cutter, or hands. Be sure to break down any large chunks of butter. Smaller pieces of butter are okay, as they will be broken down later in the process.

4. Mix buttermilk into mixture with a fork or wooden spoon until the dough is sticky and can be worked into a ball. The less mixing the better, as an overmixed dough will become tough. If dough is still dry, add additional buttermilk one tablespoon at a time.

5. Gently roll out dough on a floured surface into an 8-inch x 11-inch rectangle.

continued →

61

6   Fold the dough over onto itself, as if you are folding a cloth, about 6 times to create layers. This will help create the flaky layers within the biscuit.

7   Roll out dough into a rectangle that is about 1½ inches thick and cut circles with a floured glass or biscuit cutter. Standard biscuits are between 2 inches and 3 inches in diameter. Place biscuits on the prepared baking sheet so that the edges of the biscuits are touching.

8   Roll out scraps into a rectangle and begin the folding and cutting process again. Repeat this process until all of the dough has been used.

9   Brush a thin layer of melted butter onto the tops of the cut biscuits, if desired, and sprinkle with chives. The butter will provide more browning on the tops of the biscuits.

10 Bake biscuits for 9 to 12 minutes, or until risen and golden brown.

11 After baking, brush on an additional layer of melted butter, if desired.

Substitute any herbs and spices you choose for the chives. Other suggestions include rosemary and thyme, chives and parsley, or chives and dried onion.

Hillary Clinton

First female presidential nominee by a major US political party, secretary of state, US senator, former First Lady of the United States

"When there are no ceilings, the sky's the limit. So let's keep going—let's keep going until every one of the 161 million women and girls across America has the opportunity she deserves to have."

Jane
Goodall

Primatologist, anthropologist, humanitarian, United Nations Messenger of Peace, animal rights activist

"Every individual matters. Every individual has a role to play. Every individual makes a difference."

Jane Goodall Monkey Bread

STICKY CINNAMON MONKEY BREAD

SERVING SIZE

Serves 10 to 12

INGREDIENTS

Bread

1 cup whole milk

2 tablespoons granulated sugar

2¼ teaspoons active dry yeast (one 0.25-ounce packet)

5 tablespoons unsalted butter, melted

2 eggs

3½ cups all-purpose flour, divided

1½ teaspoons salt

Cinnamon Coating

1. **FOR THE BREAD:** In a liquid measuring cup, whisk together milk, sugar, and yeast. Allow to sit for 5 to 10 minutes, until the mixture is slightly foamy. This indicates the yeast is alive.

2. In a large mixing bowl, whisk together melted butter and eggs. Add milk mixture and whisk until combined.

3. With an electric mixer, whisk in 1½ cups of flour and the salt just until combined. Change whisk attachment to a dough hook and add the remaining 2 cups of flour. Mix with dough hook at a medium-low speed until dough forms a cohesive ball and moves as a single unit around bowl. Continue to knead for 3 additional minutes.

4. Grease a second large bowl. Remove dough and knead with hands once or twice. Transfer to greased mixing bowl and grease the top of the dough lightly with oil or cooking spray.

5. Cover bowl with plastic wrap or a towel and let sit for about 2 hours, or until dough has risen to about double in size.

6. **FOR THE CINNAMON COATING:** In a small mixing bowl, mix

continued →

BREADS

65

1 cup brown sugar

2 teaspoons ground cinnamon

5 tablespoons unsalted butter, melted

Glaze

2 cups powdered sugar

¼ cup whole milk, plus additional as needed

½ teaspoon vanilla extract

brown sugar and cinnamon and set aside. Place melted butter in a separate small bowl.

7   Lightly grease a Bundt pan. When dough is ready, lightly flour a clean work surface or piece of parchment paper. Separate the dough into 5 equal pieces and stretch each piece out to form a 10-inch log or rope. Cut each rope into 6 to 8 pieces and form each piece into a rough ball. Balls do not have to be identical.

8   Coat each ball in butter and roll in brown sugar mixture. Arrange in the Bundt pan, pressing the balls gently together as needed.

9   Cover with plastic wrap or a towel and allow to sit for 1 hour, or until balls are puffy and about doubled in size.

10 Preheat oven to 350°F.

11 Bake for 40 to 45 minutes, or until top is firm and set. Allow to sit in the Bundt pan for about 5 minutes before flipping over to remove.

12 **FOR THE GLAZE:** While monkey bread is cooling, whisk together powdered sugar, milk, and vanilla extract. Add additional milk 1 teaspoon at a time, if needed.

13 Cover the bread with glaze or serve on the side as a dipping sauce, if desired.

If you prefer, the dough can be made ahead and coated with the cinnamon coating, transferred to the Bundt pan, and set, covered, in the refrigerator for 6 to 8 hours. Allow the dough to sit at room temperature for 1 hour prior to baking.

Malala Profiterole Model

PROFITEROLES

SERVING SIZE

Makes 2 dozen
profiteroles

INGREDIENTS

Profiteroles

½ cup whole milk

½ cup water

½ cup unsalted
butter (1 stick)

1 tablespoon
granulated
sugar

¼ teaspoon salt

1 cup all-purpose
flour

4 eggs

1. Preheat oven to 425°F and line 2 baking sheets with parchment paper.

2. **FOR THE PROFITEROLES:** In a medium saucepan, stir milk, water, butter, sugar, and salt together and bring to a low boil over medium heat, stirring occasionally.

3. Pour flour directly into liquid and mix with a heat-resistant spatula or wooden spoon until dough comes together in a smooth ball, 1 to 2 minutes. Be sure to bake off all of the water to ensure light, crispy profiteroles.

4. Transfer dough to a large mixing bowl and allow to cool slightly, 5 to 10 minutes, or until steam is no longer released when mixed. When dough has cooled, beat in eggs one at a time until fully incorporated.

5. Transfer dough to a large piping bag with a 1-inch tip, or transfer to a plastic gallon storage bag and cut one corner to create a 1-inch hole.

6. Pipe mounds about 1½ inches in diameter onto parchment paper, leaving about 1 inch between each ball. Dip your finger in water and push the pointy tips down into the mounds to avoid burning.

7. Bake for 20 to 25 minutes, or until profiteroles are golden brown and about doubled in height. Allow to cool completely on baking sheets.

continued →

TRADITIONAL DESSERTS

Chocolate Sauce

½ cup heavy cream

1½ cups semisweet chocolate chips (12 ounces)

2 tablespoons maple syrup

¼ teaspoon ground cinnamon

Vanilla Ice Cream (page 79) or store-bought vanilla or coffee ice cream, for serving

8   **FOR THE CHOCOLATE SAUCE:** While profiteroles are cooling, microwave heavy cream in a microwave-safe bowl for about 45 seconds, or heat in a saucepan over low heat until just about simmering.

9   Place chocolate in a medium heatproof mixing bowl, pour hot cream over chocolate, and allow to sit for 1 to 2 minutes, or until chocolate looks soft. Whisk cream and chocolate together until smooth. Add maple syrup and cinnamon and whisk until smooth and shiny.

10   Cut profiteroles in half horizontally with a serrated knife, fill each with 1 scoop of ice cream, and top with warm chocolate sauce. Serve immediately.

Baked profiteroles can be frozen for up to 3 months. Reheat in a 375°F oven for 5 minutes.

Malala Yousafzai

Pakistani advocate for female education, youngest-ever Nobel Prize laureate, author, survivor

"I raise up my voice— not so I can shout but so that those without a voice can be heard . . . we cannot succeed when half of us are held back."

Diana, Princess of Wales

Member of the British royal family, AIDS and leprosy awareness ambassador, humanitarian

"Every one of us needs to show how much we care for each other and, in the process, care for ourselves."

Lady Diana Finger Cake

LADYFINGER ICEBOX CAKE

SERVING SIZE
Serves 10 to 12

INGREDIENTS
38 ladyfinger cookies
8 ounces mascarpone cheese
6 ounces plain full-fat Greek yogurt
¾ cup granulated sugar
2 cups heavy cream
2 teaspoons vanilla extract
½ teaspoon lemon zest
1½ cups thinly sliced strawberries, divided
¾ cup slivered almonds, divided

1. Line the bottom of a 9-inch springform pan with parchment paper.

2. Cut off the last ¼ inch of one end of 22 ladyfinger cookies to create flat ends (reserve the ¼-inch ends). Line the edge of the springform pan with the ladyfingers placed vertically, with the sugar side facing out. Place a bowl about 7 inches in diameter in the center of your pan to help balance the ladyfingers as you work around the edge if needed.

3. Fill the bottom of the pan with 8 additional ladyfingers and fill in holes with the reserved ends.

4. In a large mixing bowl, whisk together mascarpone cheese, Greek yogurt, and sugar with an electric mixer at a medium speed until smooth. Add heavy cream, vanilla extract, and lemon zest and whisk on a high speed for 3 to 5 minutes, or until stiff peaks form. The mixture will look like homemade whipped cream.

5. Scoop about half of the cream mixture into the pan and spread evenly across the ladyfingers. Fill in any holes as needed.

continued →

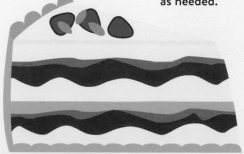

CAKES & CUPCAKES

6 Cover the cream with about ½ cup of the sliced strawberries. Sprinkle ¼ cup of the slivered almonds over the strawberries. Top strawberries and almonds with another 8 ladyfingers.

7 Cover ladyfingers with half of the remaining cream mixture and spread evenly. Top with about ½ cup of the sliced strawberries. Sprinkle ¼ cup of the almonds over the strawberries.

8 Top the strawberries with the remaining cream mixture. Top the cream with the last ½ cup of strawberries and ¼ cup of slivered almonds.

9 Cover cake with plastic wrap and place in the refrigerator for 12 hours or overnight to chill and to allow the ladyfingers to soften.

10 Remove cake from springform pan and serve cold. Store in refrigerator for up to a week.

Tarana & Milano Cookies

MILANO-STYLE COOKIES

SERVING SIZE

Makes 2 to 2½ dozen cookie sandwiches

INGREDIENTS

Cookies

2 cups all-purpose flour

½ teaspoon salt

1 cup unsalted butter, softened (2 sticks)

1½ cups granulated sugar

2 eggs

2 egg whites

1 tablespoon vanilla extract

1. Preheat oven to 325°F and line 3 to 4 baking sheets with parchment paper.

2. **FOR THE COOKIES:** In a medium mixing bowl, whisk together flour and salt. Set aside.

3. In a large mixing bowl, mix butter and sugar together with an electric mixer on medium speed until creamed. Add eggs, egg whites, and vanilla extract and mix until light and fluffy, 3 to 5 minutes.

4. Add flour about ½ cup at a time, mixing until just incorporated after each addition.

5. Transfer batter to a piping bag with a ½-inch tip, or transfer to a plastic gallon storage bag and cut one corner to create a ½-inch hole. Pipe 2-inch logs about 3 inches apart on the parchment paper.

6. Bake cookies for 15 to 20 minutes, or until bottoms of cookies are browned. Allow cookies to cool for about 5 minutes on baking sheets, then transfer to a cooling rack to finish cooling.

continued →

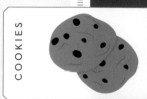

Chocolate Ganache Filling

¾ cup semisweet chocolate chips (6 ounces)

⅓ cup heavy cream

7   **FOR THE CHOCOLATE GANACHE FILLING:** While cookies are cooling, pour chocolate chips into a small mixing bowl.

8   Heat cream in a saucepan over medium-low heat until just beginning to simmer, or heat in the microwave for 45 seconds. Pour cream over the chocolate and allow to sit for 1 to 2 minutes, or until chocolate looks soft. Whisk or stir the chocolate into the cream until smooth and no chunks of chocolate remain. If needed, return to the microwave for an additional 10 seconds.

9   Allow chocolate ganache to thicken for about 2 minutes. When chocolate is ready, place ½ to 1 tablespoon of chocolate on a cookie and top with another cookie to make a sandwich. Repeat until all of the cookies are sandwiched.

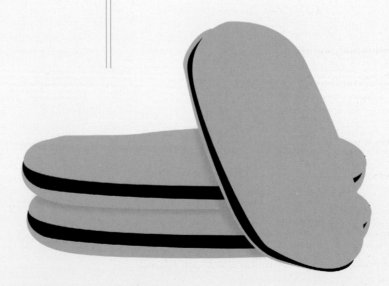

Tarana Burke and Alyssa Milano

Founders of the #Metoo movement, activists, Time magazine's 2017 Persons of the Year

"I have always tried to use my platform to educate, empower, and give people the tools to make a difference in the world."
—Alyssa Milano

Madeleine Albright

First female US secretary of state, US ambassador to the United Nations, Presidential Medal of Freedom awardee

"There is a special place in hell for women who don't help other women."

Madeleines Albright

MADELEINES

SERVING SIZE

Makes 2 dozen
madeleines

INGREDIENTS

1 cup cake flour

½ teaspoon baking
powder

3 eggs, room
temperature

¾ cup granulated
sugar

½ teaspoon salt

1 teaspoon vanilla
extract

½ teaspoon lemon
zest

10 tablespoons
unsalted butter,
melted and
cooled, plus
1 tablespoon
for greasing
the pan

1. In a medium mixing bowl, whisk together flour and baking powder. Set aside.

2. In a large mixing bowl, whisk eggs, sugar, and salt together with an electric mixer on very high speed for 10 to 15 minutes, or until egg ribbons form. The mixture will be pale and thick, and the batter will drop from the whisk like ribbons when the whisk is lifted.

3. Whisk in vanilla extract and lemon zest. Mix until combined.

4. Gently fold in half of the flour mixture and mix with a wooden spoon or spatula. Be very gentle with the batter, as the mixture has been aerated and vigorous beating will whip the air out of the batter. Repeat with the other half.

5. Pour half of the melted butter into the batter and gently fold into the batter with a wooden spoon or spatula until combined. Ensure no butter has settled at the bottom of the bowl. Repeat with the other half.

6. Cover the mixing bowl with plastic wrap and place in the refrigerator to cool for 30 minutes to 1 hour.

7. While batter is cooling, preheat oven to 375°F and melt the remaining tablespoon of butter in a small bowl. Brush melted butter into the wells of two 12-cup madeleine pans.

8. When dough has chilled, pour about 2 teaspoons of batter into the center of each madeleine well. Do not spread the batter.

9. Bake madeleines for 11 to 14 minutes, or until edges begin to brown. The cookies will rise in the center and have a small "belly."

10. Allow madeleines to cool for about 5 minutes in pans and then transfer to a cooling rack to cool completely.

11. Madeleines are best if enjoyed within 2 days.

COOKIES

Michelle Obama

Former First Lady of the United States, lawyer, author, nutrition and physical activity advocate

"The difference between a broken community and a thriving one is the presence of women who are valued."

Michelle Obama Root Beer Flotus

ROOT BEER FLOAT

SERVING SIZE

1 quart ice cream,
1 root beer float

INGREDIENTS

Vanilla Ice Cream

3 egg yolks

¾ cup granulated sugar

1½ tablespoons nonfat dry milk powder

1½ cups whole milk

1½ cups heavy whipping cream

1 tablespoon vanilla extract

Float

12 fluid ounces cold root beer

½ tablespoon chocolate sauce

1   **FOR THE VANILLA ICE CREAM:** In a medium saucepan off the heat, whisk egg yolks, sugar, and nonfat dry milk powder together until the sugar is fully dissolved.

2   In a separate medium saucepan, heat milk over medium-low heat without stirring until the milk begins to simmer on the sides and a very thin film starts to form on the top.

3   Remove milk from heat and let cool for 30 seconds. Slowly add to egg mixture while whisking continuously. Heat over medium-low heat until mixture reaches 165°F. Do not let the mixture boil.

4   Remove from heat and transfer to a storage container. Place in refrigerator and let cool until the mixture reaches at least room temperature, about 5 to 6 hours.

5   When mixture has cooled, whisk in heavy cream and vanilla extract. Transfer to an ice cream maker. Churn according to manufacturer's instructions until desired texture is reached. This can take between 20 and 50 minutes depending on the temperature of the ice cream maker and the liquid. Ice cream can be used immeadiately or stored in an airtight container in the freezer.

6   **FOR THE FLOAT:** Place two scoops of ice cream in a large glass. Pour root beer over top of ice cream. Top with chocolate sauce.

Gloria Steinem

Leader and spokeswoman for the American feminist movement, social activist, undercover journalist, author

"So whatever you want to do, just do it . . . Making a damn fool of yourself is absolutely essential."

Morning Gloria Steinem Muffins

MORNING GLORY MUFFINS

SERVING SIZE

Makes 1 to 1½ dozen muffins

INGREDIENTS

½ cup golden raisins

2 cups all-purpose flour

½ cup brown sugar

½ cup granulated sugar

2 teaspoons baking soda

1 teaspoons ground cinnamon

½ teaspoon ground ginger

¼ teaspoon ground cloves

½ teaspoon salt

3 eggs

½ cup unsalted butter, melted (1 stick)

⅓ cup orange juice

1 teaspoon orange zest

2 teaspoons vanilla extract

2 cups peeled and grated carrots

½ cup cored and grated apple

½ cup shredded sweetened coconut

½ cup walnuts

1. Preheat oven to 350°F and grease a 12-well muffin tin.

2. Place raisins in a bowl and cover with warm water to rehydrate. Set aside.

3. In a medium bowl, whisk flour, brown sugar, granulated sugar, baking soda, cinnamon, ginger, cloves, and salt together. Set aside.

4. In large mixing bowl, whisk eggs, melted butter, orange juice, orange zest, and vanilla extract together until combined.

5. Slowly add dry ingredients to the wet ingredients and mix until combined.

6. Drain and dry raisins. Add raisins, carrots, apples, coconut, and walnuts and stir with a wooden spoon or spatula until combined and evenly distributed.

7. Add batter to muffin tin, filling each well until almost full.

8. Bake muffins for 20 to 25 minutes, or until a toothpick comes out clean when inserted.

9. Let cool for about 10 minutes before removing from muffin tin.

Mother Teresa

Roman Catholic nun, founder of the Missionaries of Charity, canonized saint, Nobel Peace Prize winner

"Be faithful in small things because it is in them that your strength lies."

Mother Teresa Hot Cross Buns

HOT CROSS BUNS

SERVING SIZE

1 to 1½ dozen buns

INGREDIENTS

Buns

½ cup raisins

1 cup whole milk, warm

½ cup water, warm

2¼ teaspoons active dry yeast
(one 0.25-ounce packet)

2½ cups all-purpose flour,
plus additional as needed

2 cups bread flour

1 teaspoon baking powder

1 teaspoon ground cinnamon

½ teaspoon ground nutmeg

½ teaspoon ground cloves

½ teaspoon salt

¼ cup unsalted butter,
melted (½ stick)

2 eggs

1 teaspoon vanilla extract

½ cup granulated sugar

½ cup brown sugar

1 **FOR THE BUNS:** Place raisins in a shallow bowl and cover with water. Let sit to absorb water and rehydrate.

2 In a small bowl or liquid measuring cup, combine warm milk and water. Sprinkle yeast on top and allow to sit for 10 minutes, or until yeast starts to foam slightly. This indicates the yeast is alive.

3 While yeast is sitting, combine all-purpose flour, bread flour, baking powder, cinnamon, nutmeg, cloves, and salt. Set aside.

4 In a large mixing bowl, using an electric mixer on medium speed, whisk together melted butter, eggs, vanilla extract, sugar, and brown sugar. Add yeast and milk mixture and whisk until combined.

5 Change mixer attachment to a dough hook and add flour mixture ½ cup at a time. Knead until the dough pulls away from the sides and moves as one unit, then continue to knead for an additional 5 minutes. If the dough is too sticky, add an additonal 1 to 2 tablespoons all-purpose flour.

6 Drain and dry raisins. Add raisins to the dough and knead for 1 minute more.

continued →

BREADS

83

Egg Wash

2 tablespoons pasteurized egg whites or 1 large egg white

1 tablespoon milk (dairy or non-dairy)

Icing

½ cup powdered sugar

1½ tablespoons milk (dairy or non-dairy)

⅛ teaspoon vanilla extract

7   Transfer the dough to a greased bowl, cover with plastic wrap or a towel, and let sit for 45 minutes to 1 hour, or until dough about doubles in size.

8   Preheat oven to 375°F. Grease a 9-inch x 13-inch baking dish.

9   With greased hands, roll ⅓-cup portions of dough into balls and place onto baking dish about ½ inch apart. Cover and allow to rise for 45 minutes to 1 hour, or until dough puffs and rolls start to touch.

10   **FOR THE EGG WASH:** Whisk together egg white and milk in a small bowl and brush rolls generously with the wash. Bake for 25 to 30 minutes, or until rolls are set but bouncy and start to turn golden.

11   Allow rolls to cool completely.

12   **FOR THE ICING:** While rolls are cooling, sift powdered sugar into a medium bowl. Add milk and vanilla extract and whisk until it reaches a thick icing consistency. Place icing in a small piping bag, or transfer to a small plastic storage bag and cut one corner to create a ¼-inch hole.

13   Remove rolls from baking dish and pipe a cross of icing across each roll. (You can also spoon crosses onto the rolls if neatness is not a concern.)

14   Serve rolls warm, with butter, if desired.

Queen Lili'uokalani Pineapple Upside-Down Cake

PINEAPPLE UPSIDE-DOWN CAKE

SERVING SIZE

Serves 8 to 10

INGREDIENTS

Topping

½ cup brown sugar

¼ cup unsalted butter, melted (½ stick)

20 ounces canned pineapple slices

about 8 maraschino cherries

1 Preheat oven to 375°F and grease a 9-inch springform pan.

2 **FOR THE TOPPING:** Combine brown sugar and butter in a medium bowl and stir to mix. Spread mixture across the bottom of the greased cake pan.

3 Remove pineapple slices from can and set juices aside to use later. Arrange pineapples across the top of the brown sugar mixture. Cut Maraschino cherries in half and place one cherry half in the middle of each pineapple.

4 **FOR THE CAKE:** In a medium mixing bowl, sift together flour, baking powder, and salt. Set aside.

5 In a large mixing bowl, mix butter, sugar, and brown sugar together with an electric mixer at a medium speed until smooth. Add egg and vanilla extract and mix until combined.

6 Alternate between adding flour mixture, milk, and pineapple juice to batter, ending with flour, mixing on medium speed until combined and smooth after each addition.

continued →

Cake

1 ⅓ cups all-purpose flour

2 teaspoons baking powder

½ teaspoon salt

4 tablespoons unsalted butter, softened

½ cup granulated sugar

¼ cup brown sugar

1 egg

1 teaspoon vanilla extract

½ cup whole milk

2 tablespoons pineapple juice

7 Pour batter into cake pan and spread evenly across, covering the pineapples.

8 Place cake pan on top of a baking sheet and bake for 35 minutes, or until cake is still spongy but firm and the edges begin to brown.

9 Allow cake to cool completely in pan. When cake is cooled, place a serving plate on top of the pan and invert together. Remove the sides and top of the springform pan.

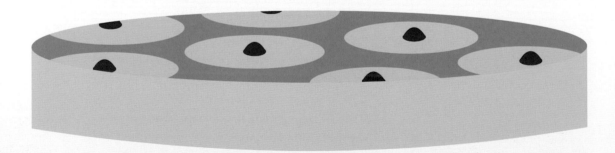

Queen Lili'uokalani

First queen and last monarch of the Kingdom of Hawaii, prisoner of the American government, author, composer

"Never cease to act because you fear you may fail."

The
Supremes

The intelligent and fierce female Supreme Court justices bring balance to a historically male Supreme Court. Celebrated in the world of law and academia, these women have reached the highest level within their profession. Each of these individuals brings knowledge and perspective that provides a greater representation of the population as a whole, such as Ginsburg's passion for women's equality and Sotomayor's personal connection with affirmative action. These women rightfully claimed their seats on the Supreme Court, just as the Supreme Diana Ross so perfectly sang: "There's my chair, I put it there."

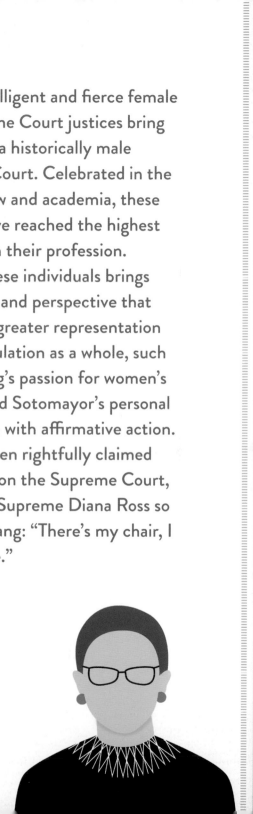

Diana Ross

Singer, actor, record producer, member of the Supremes—the best-charting girl group in US history, Presidential Medal of Freedom awardee

"You can't just sit there and wait for people to give you that golden dream. You've got to get out there and make it happen yourself."

Diana Frossted Sugar Cookies

FROSTED ALMOND SUGAR COOKIES

SERVING SIZE

Makes 2 to 3 dozen cookies

INGREDIENTS

Cookies

3 cups all-purpose flour

1 teaspoon baking powder

¼ teaspoon salt

1 cup unsalted butter, softened (2 sticks)

1 cup granulated sugar

½ teaspoon vanilla extract

½ teaspoon almond extract

1 large egg

2 teaspoons whole milk

1 **FOR THE COOKIES:** Sift flour, baking powder, and salt together in a medium mixing bowl and set aside.

2 In a large mixing bowl, mix butter, sugar, vanilla extract, and almond extract together with an electric mixer at medium speed until fluffy, 3 to 5 minutes.

3 Add egg and milk and continue to mix until combined.

4 Add flour mixture to batter in 3 additions, mixing until combined after each addition. Scrape down the sides of the bowl as needed.

5 Divide the dough in half and place each half on a floured piece of parchment paper. Roll out dough with a rolling pin until each slab is even across and about ½ inch thick.

6 Cover each dough slab with an additional piece of parchment paper and refrigerate for 30 minutes to 1 hour.

7 While dough is chilling, preheat oven to 350°F and line 2 to 3 baking sheets with parchment paper.

8 Cut chilled dough into desired shape with a cookie cutter and transfer to the lined baking sheets. Cookies will spread only minimally, so they can be positioned relatively close together.

continued →

Royal Icing

¼ cup pasteurized egg whites

¾ teaspoon vanilla extract

⅛ teaspoon almond extract

3 cups powdered sugar, sifted

Food coloring, optional

9   Bake cookies for 8 to 10 minutes, or until sides and bottoms just begin to turn golden. Allow cookies to cool on a cooling rack completely before icing.

10   **FOR THE ROYAL ICING:** While cookies are cooling, combine egg whites, vanilla extract, and almond extract in a medium mixing bowl and whisk with an electric mixer on high speed until the egg whites begin to froth.

11   Reduce the mixing speed and slowly sift powdered sugar into the egg white mixture ¼ cup at a time. Once all of the powdered sugar is added, return the mixing speed to high and mix for 5 minutes, or until icing is thick and shiny and forms stiff peaks.

12   Add food coloring, if desired, and continue to mix until color is even throughout.

13   Transfer icing to a piping bag, or transfer to a plastic gallon storage bag and cut one corner to create a ¼-inch hole. Ice cooled sugar cookies to your liking.

Ruth Bader GinsBerger Cookies

BERGER-STYLE COOKIES

SERVING SIZE

Makes 1 to 1½ dozen cookies

INGREDIENTS

Cookies

1½ cups all-purpose flour

1 teaspoon baking powder

½ teaspoon salt

6 tablespoons unsalted butter, softened

½ cup granulated sugar

1 teaspoon vanilla extract

1 egg

⅓ cup whole milk

Icing

1. Preheat oven to 375°F and line 2 baking sheets with parchment paper.

2. FOR THE COOKIES: In a medium mixing bowl whisk flour, baking powder, and salt together until combined. Set aside.

3. In a large mixing bowl, beat butter, sugar, and vanilla extract with an electric mixer at medium speed until fluffy. Add egg and milk and mix until combined.

4. Add dry ingredients to wet ingredients and mix on low speed until just combined. Be careful not to overmix, or cookies can become tough.

5. With a tablespoon or a small ice cream scoop, drop balls of dough 2 inches apart on the lined baking sheets. Press gently down on dough with your fingers or a spatula to flatten into thick disks.

6. Bake for 8 to 10 minutes, or until bottoms are just beginning to brown but tops remain light. Transfer to a cooling rack to cool.

7. FOR THE ICING: While cookies are cooling, sift powdered sugar, cocoa powder, and salt together in a medium bowl and set aside.

continued →

COOKIES

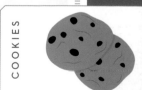

93

1 cup powdered sugar

1 tablespoon cocoa powder

⅛ teaspoon salt

⅓ cup heavy cream

1 tablespoon maple syrup

1 teaspoon vanilla extract

1 cup semisweet chocolate chips (8 ounces)

8   Whisk together heavy cream, maple syrup, and vanilla extract in a microwave-safe dish. Heat mixture in the microwave for 45 seconds, or until it begins to bubble gently along the sides. Place chocolate in a medium bowl.

9   Pour hot cream mixture over chocolate and allow to sit for 1 to 2 minutes, or until chocolate looks soft. Whisk mixture until chocolate is completely melted and smooth.

10 Whisk in powdered sugar mixture until smooth and no clumps of powdered sugar or cocoa remain.

11 Pick up cooled cookies from the bottoms and dunk into chocolate topping, allowing a generous portion to remain on the cookies.

12 Place cookies back onto baking sheets and allow chocolate to harden for at least 5 minutes.

Ruth Bader Ginsburg

Justice of the Supreme Court, judge of the US Court of Appeals, professor, gender equality advocate

"Women belong in all places where decisions are being made . . . It shouldn't be that women are the exception."

Elena
Kagan

*Justice of the US
Supreme Court, first
female solicitor general
of the US, first female
dean of Harvard Law
School*

"I have no regrets.
I don't believe in
looking back. What
I am proudest of?
Working really
hard . . . and achieving
as much as I could."

Funnelena Kagan Cake

FUNNEL CAKE

SERVING SIZE

Makes 12 large or 24 mini funnel cakes

INGREDIENTS

2 eggs

1 cup whole milk

1 cup water

1 teaspoon vanilla extract

3 cups bread flour

⅓ cup granulated sugar

1 tablespoon baking soda

½ teaspoon salt

canola or vegetable oil for frying

powdered sugar for dusting

1 In a large mixing bowl, whisk eggs until beaten.

2 Pour milk, water, and vanilla extract into eggs and whisk until combined.

3 Add flour, sugar, baking soda, and salt to mixture and whisk with an electric mixer on medium speed for 2 to 3 minutes, or until evenly combined with no large flour clumps.

4 Fill a wide-mouth saucepan about halfway with oil and heat over medium-high heat for about 5 minutes undisturbed, until the oil reaches 350°F.

5 Transfer batter to a liquid measuring cup or piping bag and pour in a spiral motion into oil, using ¼ cup at a time for individual-size funnel cakes and ⅛ cup at a time for mini. Cook for 2 to 3 minutes on each side, or until golden brown.

6 Remove with a slotted spoon and drain on a cooling rack over paper towels for about 1 minute, then sprinkle with powdered sugar and serve warm.

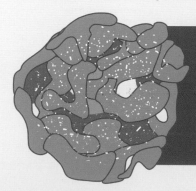

Stop to let the oil heat back up for 1 to 2 minutes after every third funnel cake. You will know the oil is hot enough if bubbles immediately form around the dough when it is poured into the pan.

Sandra Day O'Connor

First female justice of the Supreme Court, first female majority leader of a state senate, Presidential Medal of Freedom awardee

"We don't accomplish anything in this world alone . . . and whatever happens is the result of the whole tapestry of one's life and all the weavings of individual threads from one to another that creates something."

Sandra Day Oat Cobbler

APPLE AND OAT COBBLER

SERVING SIZE
Serves 8 to 10

INGREDIENTS

Filling
4 apples
⅓ cup brown sugar
1 teaspoon ground cinnamon
¼ teaspoon ground cloves
2 tablespoons whole milk

Topping
¾ cup all-purpose flour
¾ cup quick oats
¼ cup brown sugar
¼ cup granulated sugar
¼ teaspoon salt
½ cup unsalted butter, melted (1 stick)
1 teaspoon vanilla extract
⅔ cups chopped walnuts, optional

1. Preheat oven to 350°F and grease a 9-inch x 9-inch baking pan with butter or non-stick spray.

2. **FOR THE FILLING:** Peel, core, and quarter apples and slice into very thin half-moon shapes.

3. In a large mixing bowl, toss apples with brown sugar, milk, cinnamon, and cloves.

4. Pour apple mixture into prepared pan and bake for 15 minutes.

5. **FOR THE TOPPING:** While apples are baking, mix flour, oats, brown sugar, granulated sugar, salt, melted butter, vanilla extract, and walnuts, if desired, with a wooden spoon or spatula until combined.

6. Pour topping over baked apples and press the topping down gently with your fingertips or a spatula.

7. Return to the oven and bake for 1 hour, or until oat topping is golden and apples are soft when poked with a toothpick or knife.

8. Serve warm with a dollop of ice cream, if desired.

Sonia Sotomayor

First Supreme Court justice of Hispanic descent, judge of the US Court of Appeals, professor

"I do know one thing about me: I don't measure myself by others' expectations or let others define my worth."

Sonia SotoMeyer Lemon Squares

MEYER LEMON SQUARES

SERVING SIZE

Makes 1½ to 2 dozen squares

INGREDIENTS

Crust

¾ cup all-purpose flour

½ cup powdered sugar

¼ cup cornstarch

¾ teaspoon salt

6 tablespoons
unsalted butter, cubed

Lemon Topping

3 large eggs

1¼ cups granulated sugar

¼ cup all-purpose flour

1½ tablespoons Meyer lemon
zest

6 tablespoons Meyer lemon
juice (from 3 to 4
Meyer lemons)

½ teaspoon vanilla extract

powdered sugar, for topping

1   Preheat oven to 350°F. Cover a 9-inch x 9-inch baking pan, including sides, in parchment paper and grease well with butter or cooking spray.

2   **FOR THE CRUST:** Combine flour, powdered sugar, cornstarch, and salt and whisk in a medium mixing bowl until combined.

3   Cut in cubes of butter and work into mixture with a fork, a whisk, or your hands until the mixture forms small crumbs.

4   Press crust mixture firmly down into bottom of prepared pan until it is spread evenly. Refrigerate crust for 10 minutes.

5   Bake chilled crust for 15 to 20 minutes, or until slightly golden.

6   **FOR THE LEMON TOPPING:** In a medium bowl, whisk eggs until beaten, then add sugar, flour, Meyer lemon zest, lemon juice, and vanilla extract and whisk until combined.

7   Pour lemon filling onto crust and return to the oven to bake for 20 to 25 minutes, or until the top is firm and edges are slightly browned.

8   Let the lemon squares cool to room temperature in the pan, then place in the refrigerator for 30 minutes to one hour.

9   When chilled and ready to cut, remove parchment from square pan and sift powdered sugar onto the bars (as much as you please).

10 Cut lemon squares into 2-inch-square pieces.

Trailblazers

Trailblazing women have stood tall in the face of doubt and bigotry, paving the way for the next generation. Many of these bold women were pioneers in their industries and achieved historical firsts. Sally Ride was the first woman in space, Barbara Walters was the first female coanchor of network evening news, and Ellen DeGeneres portrayed the first openly gay lead character in a network sitcom. Unabashed and unafraid, they explored uncharted territory. These women opened doors, studios, closets, and galaxies for women all over the world.

Annie Oakley

*Sharpshooter,
American cowgirl,
performer, advocate for
female empowerment*

"Aim at a high mark
and you will hit it. No,
not the first time,
nor the second and
maybe not the third.
But keep on aiming
and keep on shooting
for only practice will
make you perfect.
Finally, you'll hit the
Bull's Eye of Success."

Annie Oatley Granola

VANILLA ALMOND GRANOLA

SERVING SIZE

Makes 4 cups

INGREDIENTS

2 ¾ cups old-fashioned oats

1 cup sliced almonds

⅓ cup brown sugar

2 tablespoons ground flaxseed

¼ teaspoon salt

¼ cup refined coconut oil, melted

3 tablespoons maple syrup

1 tablespoon vanilla extract

½ cup dried fruit, optional

1. Preheat oven to 350°F and line a large baking sheet with parchment paper.

2. Combine oats, almonds, brown sugar, flaxseed, and salt in a large bowl and mix until evenly distributed.

3. Add melted coconut oil, maple syrup, and vanilla extract to oats and fold into oat mixture with a wooden spoon or spatula until every oat is coated.

4. Pour mixture evenly onto the prepared baking sheet and bake for 20 to 25 minutes, or until golden and fragrant. If you prefer clustery granola, do not mix while baking. If you prefer more oat-like granola, remove the pan halfway through baking and break apart any clusters with a wooden spoon.

5. Cool to room temperature on baking sheet. Once granola is cool, mix in dried fruit, if desired.

6. Store in an airtight container and serve with milk, yogurt, or vanilla ice cream, if desired.

Barbara Walters

First female cohost of an American news program, first female coanchor of a network evening news show, Emmy Award–winning talk show host, broadcast journalist, executive producer

―――――

"I've always wanted to do a show with women of different generations, backgrounds, and views: a working mother, a professional in her thirties, a young woman just starting out, and then somebody who's done almost everything and will say almost anything. And in a perfect world, I'd get to join the group whenever I wanted."

Barbara Waltersmelon Popsicles

WATERMELON MINT POPSICLES

SERVING SIZE

Makes 6 popsicles

INGREDIENTS

2 cups cubed watermelon

¼ cup water

1 tablespoon agave syrup

1 tablespoon granulated sugar

2 teaspoons chopped fresh mint leaves

⅛ teaspoon salt

1   Combine all ingredients in a blender and blend until smooth.

2   Pour ingredients into popsicle molds until full. Insert popsicle sticks and seal with popsicle mold cap or aluminum foil.

3   Freeze popsicle molds for 6 to 8 hours, or until completely frozen.

4   Remove from popsicle molds and enjoy.

This recipe can also be made in ice cube trays if a popsicle mold is not available. Watermelon mint ice cubes can be added to seltzer or lemonade for an extra kick.

Amelia Earhart

First female aviator to fly solo across the Atlantic Ocean, advocate and mentor for female pilots, author

"The most difficult thing is the decision to act. The rest is merely tenacity."

Chamamelia Earhart Cupcakes

CHAMOMILE AND HONEY CUPCAKES

continued →

SERVING SIZE

Makes 2 to 2½ dozen cupcakes

INGREDIENTS

Cupcakes

2 cups all-purpose flour

½ teaspoon salt

1 cup unsalted butter, softened (2 sticks)

1½ cups granulated sugar

3 tablespoons chamomile tea leaves (from 6 chamomile tea bags)

2½ teaspoons baking powder

1 teaspoon lemon zest

1½ teaspoons vanilla extract

3 eggs

½ cup brewed chamomile tea, cooled to room temperature

½ cup heavy cream

1   Preheat oven to 350°F and line two cupcake tins with cupcake liners.

2   FOR THE CUPCAKES: In a medium mixing bowl, sift or whisk flour and salt together and set aside.

3   In a large mixing bowl, mix butter, sugar, chamomile leaves, baking powder, lemon zest, and vanilla extract together with an electric mixer on medium speed until fluffy, about 5 minutes.

4   Add eggs one at a time, mixing until combined after each addition.

5   Alternate between adding flour mixture and heavy cream to the batter. Mix on medium-low speed until combined between each addition.

6   Pour batter into cupcake tins and fill each well about three-quarters full. Bake for 20 to 25 minutes, or until edges start to brown and a toothpick comes out clean when inserted.

Frosting

½ cup unsalted butter (1 stick)

4 cups powdered sugar

2 tablespoons honey

3 tablespoons milk (dairy or non-dairy), plus additional as needed

½ teaspoon vanilla extract

7   **FOR THE FROSTING:** While cupcakes are cooling, beat butter with an electric mixer on high speed until fluffy, about 3 minutes.

8   Add powdered sugar, honey, milk, and vanilla extract to butter. If frosting is too thick, add additional milk 1 teaspoon at a time until desired texture is reached.

9   Once cupcakes are fully cooled, transfer frosting to a large piping bag with a ½-inch tip, or transfer to a plastic gallon storage bag and cut one corner to create a ½-inch hole. Pipe frosting onto cupcakes in style of your choice.

Where to buy chamomile?

Chamomile tea bags are the most common and often cheapest source of chamomile leaves available. When buying chamomile tea, look for products that list chamomile as the only ingredient.

Sarah Breedlove Millionaire Bars

THREE-LAYER MILLIONAIRE BARS

SERVING SIZE

Makes 16 to
24 bars

INGREDIENTS

**Shortbread
Crust**

¾ cup all-purpose
flour

½ cup brown sugar

¼ cup cornstarch

¼ teaspoon salt

7 tablespoons
cold unsalted
butter, cubed

1   Preheat oven to 350°F and line an 8-inch x 8-inch
pan with parchment paper, including sides.

2   FOR THE SHORTBREAD CRUST: In a large mixing
bowl, whisk flour, brown sugar, cornstarch, and salt
together. Cut in butter and work together with your
hands, a wooden spoon, or a fork until mixture is
loose and crumbly.

3   Press crust firmly into bottom of baking pan with
your hands and bake for 22 to 25 minutes, or until
crust is golden around the edges.

4   FOR THE CARAMEL LAYER: Combine sweetened
condensed milk, butter, brown sugar, agave, and
vanilla extract in a large microwave-safe bowl and
whisk to combine. Microwave for 7 to 8 minutes,
stopping to whisk thoroughly every 30 seconds.
Continue until the mixture is thick and a rich
caramel color. The last few times you mix the
caramel it will steam and have the structure of a
beehive as you begin to mix.

5   When the caramel is ready, pour on top of the
shortbread layer and allow to cool for 15 minutes.

continued →

BROWNIES
& BARS

Caramel Layer

14 ounces sweetened condensed milk

6 tablespoons unsalted butter

2 tablespoons dark brown sugar

2 tablespoons agave syrup

1 teaspoon vanilla extract

Chocolate Ganache

¼ cup heavy cream

¾ cup semisweet chocolate chips (6 ounces)

sea salt for topping

6   **FOR THE CHOCOLATE GANACHE:** Heat heavy cream in a microwave-safe bowl for about 45 seconds, or until just about simmering.

7   Place chocolate in a medium bowl. Pour cream over chocolate and allow to sit for about 1 minute, or until chocolate looks soft. Whisk cream and chocolate together until smooth and shiny.

8   Pour chocolate on top of the cool caramel, spreading evenly with a spatula or the back of a spoon. Sprinkle sea salt on top and set in the refrigerator for 1 hour to allow chocolate to harden.

9   Once completely cool, remove the bars by lifting the parchment paper out of the pan. Set on a cutting board and cut into 16 or 24 bars.

Sarah Breedlove

First female self-made millionaire in the US, philanthropist, social activist, pioneer of the modern black hair care and cosmetic industry

"I got my start by giving myself a start."

Ellen DeGeneres

First actor to star as an openly gay character on prime-time TV, television host, LGBTQ+ activist, humanitarian, Presidential Medal of Freedom awardee

"Follow your passion. Stay true to yourself. Never follow someone else's path unless you're in the woods and you're lost and you see a path. By all means, you should follow that."

Ellenphant Ears

SPICED ELEPHANT EARS

SERVING SIZE

Makes 2 dozen elephant ears

INGREDIENTS

¾ cup granulated sugar

½ teaspoon ground cinnamon

¼ teaspoon ground ginger

¼ teaspoon ground cloves

⅛ teaspoon salt

1 sheet frozen puff pastry, thawed, or 1 recipe puff pastry from Mia Hamm and Cheese Foldovers (page 181) followed through step 8

1. In a small mixing bowl, whisk together sugar, cinnamon, ginger, cloves, and salt.

2. Spread half of the spiced sugar mixture on a clean work surface or parchment paper, then unfold pastry sheet on top of the sugar mixture.

3. Top pastry sheet with the remaining spiced sugar mixture. Lay a piece of parchment paper on top of pastry sheet and roll puff pastry out to a 12-inch x 12-inch square.

4. Remove parchment paper and put any displaced sugar mixture back onto the top or bottom of puff pastry, pushing the sugar gently in with the palm of your hand as needed.

5. Fold the last two inches of two opposite sides of the square over onto the puff pastry, so that the ends are halfway to the center. Fold over again so that the folds from either side meet in the center. Fold one more time where the sides meet, laying one side on top of the other, to create a 2-inch x 12-inch rectangle.

6. Wrap pastry gently in parchment paper and place in the refrigerator for 30 minutes to allow the dough to become firm.

7. Preheat oven to 450°F and line 2 baking sheets with parchment paper.

continued →

COOKIES

115

8   Cut chilled dough into ½-inch slices with a serrated knife and place on baking sheets cut side down. Leave about 1 inch between each elephant ear because the sides will butterfly out during baking.

9   Bake for 6 minutes, then carefully flip and bake for 5 minutes more. Allow elephant ears to cool completely on pan.

Other spices can be substituted for the cinnamon, ginger, and cloves according to your preference. We recommend 1 teaspoon chai spice, 1 teaspoon pumpkin spice, or ½ teaspoon allspice.

Sheryl Sandberg Lean Instant Coffee Cake

INSTANT COFFEE CAKE

SERVING SIZE

Serves 8 to 10

INGREDIENTS

Cake

2¼ cups all-purpose flour

1 teaspoon baking soda

1 teaspoon baking powder

¼ teaspoon salt

1 cup granulated sugar

½ cup unsalted butter, softened (1 stick)

1 teaspoon vanilla extract

2 eggs

½ cup brewed and cooled instant coffee

1. Preheat oven to 350°F and grease a 9-inch x 5-inch x 3-inch loaf pan.

2. **FOR THE CAKE:** In a medium mixing bowl, sift together flour, baking soda, baking powder, and salt. Set aside.

3. In a large mixing bowl, mix sugar, butter, and vanilla extract with an electric mixer on medium speed until combined. Add eggs one at a time, mixing on medium speed until combined after each addition.

4. Alternate between adding flour mixture and coffee to wet ingredients, mixing on low speed until combined after each addition.

5. Pour half of the batter into prepared baking dish and set the other half aside.

6. **FOR THE CINNAMON FILLING:** In a medium mixing bowl, whisk together melted butter, brown sugar, instant coffee, and cinnamon. Pour mixture over the batter in the baking dish, then cover with the remaining cake batter.

continued →

Cinnamon Filling

4 tablesppons unsalted butter, melted

⅓ cup packed brown sugar

2 teaspoons instant coffee granules

1 teaspoon ground cinnamon

Topping

3 tablespoons unsalted butter, melted

½ cup all-purpose flour

¼ cup packed brown sugar

2 teaspoons ground cinnamon

1 teaspoon instant coffee granules

7   **FOR THE TOPPING:** In a separate medium mixing bowl, mix melted butter, flour, brown sugar, cinnamon, and instant coffee with a wooden spoon or spatula until it forms a ball.

8   Break the topping apart with your fingers and sprinkle on top of the batter.

9   Bake for 50 minutes, or until a wooden toothpick comes out clean when inserted. Allow to cool completely before removing from pan to serve.

Sheryl Sandberg

American technology executive, author, advocate for female leadership and empowerment

"In the future, there will be no female leaders. There will just be leaders."

Florence Nightingale

Founder of modern nursing, founder of the first secular nursing school, social reformer, statistician

"I attribute my success to this—I never gave or took an excuse."

Florentines Nightingale

COCONUT FLORENTINES

SERVING SIZE

Makest 3 dozen cookies

INGREDIENTS

Cookies

1¾ cups quick oats

1 cup granulated sugar

⅔ cup all-purpose flour

⅓ cup shredded unsweetened coconut

10 tablespoons unsalted butter, melted

⅓ cup agave syrup

⅓ cup whole milk or coconut milk

1 teaspoon vanilla extract

¼ teaspoon salt

Chocolate Coating

1 cup semisweet chocolate chips

2 teaspoons unrefined coconut oil

1. Preheat oven to 375°F and line baking sheets with aluminum foil.

2. **FOR THE COOKIES:** In a large mixing bowl, mix oats, sugar, flour, coconut, melted butter, agave syrup, milk, vanilla extract, and salt until combined.

3. While dough is still warm or room temperature, drop dough by teaspoonfuls onto baking sheets about 3 inches apart and spread thinly with a spatula or hands. (We recommend alternating between 2 cookies per row and 1 cookie per row to allow cookies enough space.)

4. Bake each batch for 8 to 10 minutes or until entirely golden brown, then allow to cool completely on foil.

5. **FOR THE CHOCOLATE COATING:** While cookies are cooling, melt semisweet chocolate in a double boiler over low heat or in the microwave at 30-second intervals, stirring between each interval. Mix coconut oil into chocolate until smooth.

6. Once the cookies are completely cool, peel from the foil and dip bottom of each cookie into chocolate. Flip over and place back on the foil to allow chocolate to harden for at least 5 minutes.

121

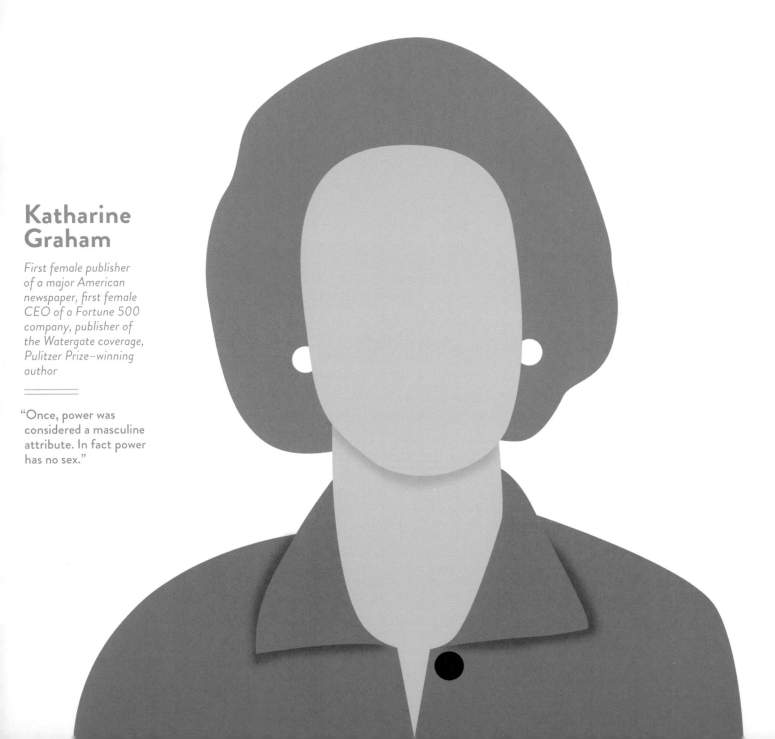

Katharine Graham

First female publisher of a major American newspaper, first female CEO of a Fortune 500 company, publisher of the Watergate coverage, Pulitzer Prize–winning author

"Once, power was considered a masculine attribute. In fact power has no sex."

Katharine Graham Cracker Crust

GRAHAM CRACKER CRUST

SERVING SIZE

Makes 1 pie crust

INGREDIENTS

1½ cups graham cracker crumbs (from 10 to 12 crackers)

½ cup butter, melted (1 stick), plus additional as needed

¼ cup brown sugar

¼ teaspoon salt

1. Preheat oven to 350°F and grease an 8-inch pie pan.

2. In a large mixing bowl, mix graham cracker crumbs, melted butter, brown sugar, and salt with an electric mixer on low speed. Mixture should be loose, but stick together when pressed between fingers. If the mixture is too dry, add an additional tablespoon of melted butter.

3. Press graham cracker mixture into the greased pie pan and bake for 8 minutes, or until lightly golden.

4. Remove graham cracker crust from the oven. Crust is completely baked and can be filled with the ready-to-eat topping of your choice, or can be filled with a topping and baked for up to 15 to 20 minutes more.

Mary Tyler Moore

Emmy Award–winning actor, produced and starred in the first sitcom built around a female character's working life, SAG Lifetime Achievement awardee, animal rights activist

"Having a dream is what keeps you alive. Overcoming the challenges makes life worth living."

Mary Tyler S'moores Pie

S'MORES PIE

SERVING SIZE

Serves 8 to 10

INGREDIENTS

1 recipe Katharine Graham Cracker Crust (page 123), or 1 store-bought graham cracker crust

¾ cup milk chocolate chips or squares (6 ounces)

⅓ cup pasteurized egg whites

⅛ teaspoon salt

¼ cup sugar

1 cup marshmallow crème

1. Preheat oven to 350°F and position rack in middle third of the oven. Ensure that the pie tin will be *at least* 12 inches away from the top of the oven.

2. Bake graham cracker crust according to recipe instructions, or if using store-bought crust, place in the oven for 5 minutes to warm.

3. Remove graham cracker crust from the oven, immediately top with an even layer of milk chocolate squares or chips, and allow chocolate to melt.

4. While chocolate is melting, beat egg whites and salt together with an electric mixer on high speed until foamy and small white bubbles appear.

5. Add sugar, 1 tablespoon at a time, and continue to beat on high speed until stiff, glossy peaks form. This will take about 5 minutes.

6. Place marshmallow crème in a separate bowl and gently mix in egg white mixture ½ cup at a time with a wooden spoon or spatula. Be careful not to overmix and collapse the egg whites.

7. Pour and spread marshmallow meringue evenly onto pie crust. You can form peaks using a whisk to twist and lift the meringue.

8. Return pie to oven and broil for 2 to 3 minutes, until marshmallow crème browns slightly. Monitor pie during broil process and remove immediately when browned as marshmallow pie can burn quickly.

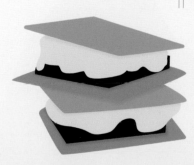

PIES TARTS & COBBLERS

Marie Curie

First woman to win a Nobel Prize, first person to win the Nobel Prize twice, chemist, physicist, discovered radium and polonium

"One never notices what has been done; one can only see what remains to be done."

Marie Curied Cashew Cups

CHOCOLATE CURRY CASHEW BUTTER CUPS

SERVING SIZE

Makes 1 dozen chocolate cups

INGREDIENTS

¾ cup semisweet chocolate squares, divided (6 ounces)

4 teaspoons unrefined coconut oil, divided, plus additional as needed

½ cup roasted, unsalted cashews

1 tablespoon honey

½ teaspoon curry powder

⅛ teaspoon sea salt, plus more for sprinkling

12 cashew halves, optional

1. Line a 12-well mini cupcake tin with liners or arrange 12 mini cupcake liners close together on a plate.

2. Melt 3 ounces of semisweet chocolate in a double boiler over low heat, or microwave in a medium microwave-safe bowl in 30-second intervals, stirring between each interval. Stir in 1½ teaspoons coconut oil until combined and smooth.

3. Pour about 1 teaspoon chocolate into each mini cupcake well. Set in the refrigerator to harden.

4. Combine 1 teaspoon coconut oil, cashews, honey, curry powder, and salt in a food processor or high-speed blender. Pulse until a smooth peanut butter–like consistency is reached. Patience is needed, as this can take 5 to 10 minutes. Stop every 1 to 2 minutes to scrape down the sides. If cashews are not reaching a smooth state after 10 minutes, add additional coconut oil 1 teaspoon at a time and pulse until smooth.

5. Remove chocolate cups from refrigerator. Scoop about ½ teaspoon curry cashew butter into each well and press down into an even disk, leaving a small space around the sides.

continued →

6   Melt the remaining 3 ounces semisweet chocolate in a double boiler over low heat, or microwave in a medium microwave-safe bowl in 30-second intervals, stirring between each interval. Stir in remaining 1½ teaspoons of coconut oil until combined and smooth.

7   Top each chocolate cup with an additional 1 teaspoon of chocolate, pressing down with a spoon if needed to completely cover sides.

8   Top each cup with a cashew half, sea salt, or both, if desired.

9   Place chocolate cups in the refrigerator for 30 minutes to set.

The unrefined coconut oil gives the cashew cups a light coconut taste; you can substitute refined if you prefer no coconut flavor.

Shonda Rhimes TGITiramisu

TIRAMISU

TIRAMISU

SERVING SIZE

Serves 8 to 10

INGREDIENTS

Ladyfinger Base

About 20 ladyfinger cookies

¾ cup brewed espresso, cooled

1 tablespoon amaretto

2 teaspoons vanilla extract

1 tablespoon granulated sugar

2 teaspoons cocoa powder

Cream

½ cup pasteurized egg whites

¼ cup plus 1½ tablespoons granulated sugar, divided

3 egg yolks

2 tablespoons amaretto

8 ounces mascarpone cheese

1¼ teaspoons cocoa powder, divided

1. **FOR THE LADYFINGER BASE:** To measure how many cookies you will need for each layer, line an 8-inch x 8-inch dish with ladyfingers, cutting cookies into halves or pieces as necessary to fill the entire bottom. Remove cookies and repeat with a second set of cookies. Remove cookies and set all of the cookies aside.

2. In a shallow, flat-bottomed bowl, whisk cooled espresso, amaretto, vanilla extract, sugar, and cocoa until combined. Set aside.

3. **FOR THE CREAM:** Combine egg whites and 1½ tablespoons of the sugar in a medium mixing bowl. Whisk with an electric mixer on high speed until stiff peaks form, about 5 minutes. Set aside.

4. In a small saucepan, combine egg yolks, remaining ¼ cup sugar, and the amaretto. Whisk constantly by hand or with an electric mixer on low speed over low heat for about 10 minutes, or until thick and pale yellow in color. Do not let the egg mixture start to boil.

5. Transfer egg yolk mixture to a large mixing bowl and gently fold in egg white mixture in thirds, mixing gently until all of the egg white mixture is combined.

continued →

TRADITIONAL DESSERTS

129

6   Add mascarpone cheese to cream and mix in gently until combined. Set cream aside.

7   Dip half of the ladyfingers into espresso mixture for about 2 seconds, quickly flipping 2 to 3 times, and line the bottom of the pan with them.

8   Top cookies with half of the cream, and sift about ¼ teaspoon cocoa powder over the top.

9   Dip the second half of the ladyfingers into espresso mixture and make a second cookie layer on top of the cream. Top cookies with remaining cream, and sift about ½ teaspoon cocoa powder over the cream.

10 Cover with plastic wrap and refrigerate for 6 to 8 hours. Dust with an additional ½ teaspoon of cocoa powder immediately before serving.

Shonda Rhimes

Television producer, screenwriter, first African American woman to produce a top-ten network series, executive producer of nine prime-time TV series

"I'm a black woman every day, and I'm not confused about that. I'm not worried about that. I don't need to have a discussion with you about how I feel as a black woman, because I don't feel disempowered as a black woman."

Sally Ride

First female American astronaut in space, Presidential Medal of Freedom awardee, physicist, engineer, cofounder of Sally Ride Science

"Young girls need to see role models in whatever careers they may choose, just so they can picture themselves doing those jobs someday. You can't be what you can't see."

Sally Ride Moon Pies

PEANUT BUTTER MOON PIES

SERVING SIZE

Makes 1½ to 2 dozen cookie sandwiches

INGREDIENTS

Cookies

1 cup unsalted butter, softened

¾ cup granulated sugar

2 teaspoons vanilla extract

1¾ cups all-purpose flour

½ cup graham cracker crumbs

¾ teaspoon salt

Filling

1 cup marshmallow crème

½ cup peanut butter

Chocolate Coating:

1½ cups chocolate melting wafers (12 ounces)

1. **FOR THE COOKIES:** In a large mixing bowl, mix butter and sugar together with an electric mixer on a medium speed until fluffy, about 3 minutes. Add vanilla extract and mix until combined.

2. Add flour, graham cracker crumbs, and salt and continue to mix on medium speed until just combined.

3. Place dough between two pieces of parchment or wax paper and roll out to a ¼-to-½-inch slab. Refrigerate dough for at least 1 hour.

4. Preheat oven to 350°F and line 2 to 3 baking sheets with parchment paper.

5. With a cookie cutter or small floured glass, cut dough into circles that are 1 to 1½ inches in diameter and transfer to lined baking sheets. Bake for 10 to 15 minutes, or until bottoms begin to brown. Allow cookies to cool completely on a cooling rack.

6. **FOR THE FILLING:** While cookies are cooling, whisk marshmallow crème and peanut butter together with an electric mixer on high speed. Spread 1 to 2 teaspoons of the filling across half of the cookies and top each with an additional cookie to make a sandwich. Allow cookie sandwiches to set for about 5 minutes.

7. **FOR THE CHOCOLATE COATING:** Melt chocolate in the microwave at 30-second intervals, stirring between each interval, or in a double boiler while stirring constantly, until chocolate is fully melted.

8. Dunk cookies into melted chocolate, covering the top and part of the sides. Place on parchment paper or wax paper and allow chocolate to drip down the remainder of the sides. Allow cookies to sit for about 15 minutes for chocolate to harden.

9. Store cookies in the refrigerator and serve cold or at room temperature.

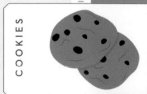

Artists & Creators

Until recently, to be taken seriously as artists, women had to disguise their identities with initials and pseudonyms. Even when brilliant woman like Zelda Fitzgerald, Frida Kahlo, and Kathryn Bigelow presented their art undisguised, it was still referred to at times as "the work of a brilliant man's wife." Women have created movies that made us cry, penned books that made us laugh, and designed clothes that perfectly balanced our power and femininity. They have made our world more beautiful, empathetic, and connected, while working twice as hard to be taken seriously.

Tina Fey and Amy Poehler

Actors, writers, comedians, producers, first female SNL Weekend Update coanchors

"Bitches get stuff done."

Amy & Tina's Weekend UpDate & Nut Balls

DATE AND NUT BALLS

SERVING SIZE
Makes 18 to 24 balls

INGREDIENTS
1½ cups dates, pitted and chopped

1¼ cups chopped walnuts

¾ cup unsweetened shredded coconut flakes

½ cup chopped almonds

1 tablespoon unsweetened cocoa powder

1 tablespoon whiskey, plus additional as needed

¼ teaspoon vanilla extract

¼ cup powdered sugar, optional

¼ cup sweetened shredded coconut flakes, optional

1. Combine dates, walnuts, unsweetened coconut, almonds, cocoa powder, whiskey, and vanilla extract in a large food processor.

2. Pulse until ingredients are broken down and form into a rough clump, rolling as one unit around the food processor.

3. Taste and add an additional tablespoon of whiskey, if desired.

4. Roll 1-tablespoon portions into 1-inch balls with hands.

5. Roll to coat in coconut flakes and/or powdered sugar, if desired.

Anna Wintour

British American journalist, editor-in-chief of Vogue, trustee and benefits chair of the Metropolitan Museum of Art

"It's very important to take risks. I think that research is very important, but in the end you have to work from your instinct and feeling and take those risks and be fearless."

Anna Wintorte

FLOURLESS CHOCOLATE TORTE

SERVING SIZE

Serves 12 to 14

INGREDIENTS

1 cup semisweet chocolate squares (8 ounces)

½ cup unsalted butter (1 stick)

1½ cups granulated sugar

5 eggs

1 tablespoon heavy cream

1 teaspoon vanilla extract

¼ teaspoon almond extract

2 tablespoons cocoa powder

1 Preheat oven to 375°F and line a 10-inch springform pan with parchment paper. Grease pan entirely, including sides.

2 Melt chocolate and butter in a large microwave-safe bowl in 30-second intervals, stirring between each interval, or in a medium saucepan over low heat, stirring constantly, until shiny and smooth.

3 Transfer chocolate and butter to a large mixing bowl. Whisk in sugar by hand or with an electric mixer at a low speed until combined.

4 Add eggs, mixing until combined between each addition.

5 Add heavy cream, vanilla extract, and almond extract and mix until combined.

6 Sift cocoa powder into a small bowl, then mix into batter until combined.

7 Pour batter into prepared pan and place pan on a large baking sheet.

8 Bake for 45 to 50 minutes, or until edges are set but center is still slightly loose.

9 Allow cake to cool for at least 20 minutes in the pan. Run a sharp knife along the edge between the cake and pan, then release from the springform pan.

10 Top with powdered sugar, berries, whipped cream, or more cocoa powder for serving.

Coco
Chanel

*Designer, entrepreneur,
fashion icon, credited
with liberating
women's clothing
from constraining
silhouettes.*

"The most courageous
act is still to think for
yourself. Aloud."

Coconut Chanel Macaroons

COCONUT MACAROONS

SERVING SIZE

Makes 1 to 1½ dozen macaroons

INGREDIENTS

1 ⅓ cups sweetened shredded coconut flakes

½ cup granulated sugar

3 tablespoons all-purpose flour

1 teaspoon vanilla extract

⅛ teaspoon almond extract

¼ cup pasteurized egg whites

⅛ teaspoon salt

1. Preheat oven to 325°F and line 1 to 2 baking sheets with parchment paper.

2. In a medium mixing bowl, whisk together coconut, sugar, flour, vanilla extract, and almond extract until combined.

3. In a separate large bowl, whisk together egg whites and salt with an electric mixer on high speed until stiff peaks form, about 5 minutes.

4. With a wooden spoon or spatula, gently fold coconut mixture into egg white mixture until combined.

5. Drop by rounded tablespoons 1 inch apart on baking sheet.

6. Bake for 20 minutes, or until tops and edges are golden.

7. Allow macaroons to cool completely on baking sheet.

COOKIES

Frida
Kahlo

*Artist, surrealist,
Mexican political
activist, teacher*

———————

"I am my own muse,
I am the subject I
know best. I am the
subject I want to
know better."

Frida Kahlúa Cupcakes

KAHLÚA AND CHOCOLATE CUPCAKES

Makes 1½ to 2 dozen cupcakes

INGREDIENTS

Cupcakes

1¼ cups all-purpose flour

⅓ cup unsweetened cocoa powder

1 teaspoon baking soda

½ teaspoon baking powder

½ teaspoon salt

1 cup granulated sugar

½ cup unsalted butter, softened (1 stick)

1 egg

½ cup brewed coffee, cooled

½ cup Kahlúa

1 teaspoon vanilla extract

1. Preheat oven to 350°F and line two 12-well cupcake tins with liners.

2. **FOR THE CUPCAKES:** Whisk flour, cocoa powder, baking soda, baking powder, and salt together in a medium mixing bowl. Set aside.

3. In a large mixing bowl, mix sugar and butter with an electric mixer on medium speed until light and fluffy, about 5 minutes, scraping down the sides with a spatula as needed.

4. Add egg and mix until incorporated. Slowly add coffee, Kahlúa, and vanilla extract. Mix until combined.

5. Add flour mixture about ⅓ cup at a time, mixing on low speed until combined between each addition.

6. Pour batter into cupcake liners until each is about three-quarters full and transfer to oven to bake for 15 to 20 minutes, or until a toothpick comes out clean when inserted.

7. Allow cupcakes to cool slightly in the pan, then transfer to a cooling rack to cool completely.

continued →

CAKES & CUPCAKES

Frosting

6 tablespoons unsalted butter, softened

1½ cups powdered sugar

1 to 2 tablespoons Kahlúa

⅛ teaspoon vanilla extract

milk (dairy or non-dairy), as needed

8   **FOR THE FROSTING:** While cupcakes are cooling, place butter in a medium mixing bowl and beat with an electric mixer on medium speed until fluffy.

9   Sift powdered sugar into the butter and continue to beat on high speed while slowly adding in Kahlúa and vanilla extract. If the frosting is too thick to spread easily, add milk 1 teaspoon at a time until desired consistency is reached.

10 Transfer frosting to a large piping bag, or transfer to a plastic gallon storage bag and cut one corner to create a ½-inch hole. Swirl a dollop of frosting onto each cupcake.

Georgia O'Keeffe Lime Pie Tartlets

KEY LIME PIE TARTLETS

SERVING SIZE

Makes 12 tartlets

INGREDIENTS

Tartlets

1 recipe Katharine Graham Cracker Crust (page 123), prepared through step 3

4 egg yolks

14 ounces sweetened condensed milk

½ cup fresh key lime juice (from 15 to 20 key limes)

2 teaspoons key lime zest

2 tablespoons nonfat dry milk

1. Preheat oven to 350°F. and grease a 12-well muffin tin. For this recipe, a silicone muffin tin will work best.

2. **FOR THE TARTLETS:** Prepare Katharine Graham Cracker Crust. Drop about 2 tablespoons crust mixture into each muffin well and press down firmly. Ensure the crust completely covers the bottom and goes about ½ inch up the sides.

3. Place a cupcake liner onto each crust and fill with rice, baking weights, or beans to prevent crust from rising during baking. Bake crusts for 8 minutes. Remove from the oven and leave oven on.

4. In a large mixing bowl, whisk egg yolks with an electric mixer on high speed until doubled in size and pale yellow in color, 5 to 10 minutes.

5. Slowly add sweetened condensed milk and mix on low speed until combined.

6. Add key lime juice, lime zest, and nonfat dry milk and mix on medium-low speed until combined.

continued →

145

Whipped Cream

½ cup heavy whipping cream

1½ tablespoons sugar

7   Divide batter evenly among the 12 crusts and bake for 15 minutes, or until centers are set. Allow tartlets to cool completely in muffin tin then transfer to a cooling rack or serving tray to be topped.

8   **FOR THE WHIPPED CREAM:** While tartlets are cooling, whisk heavy whipping cream and sugar together with an electric mixer on high speed until stiff peaks are formed, about 5 minutes.

9   When tartlets are completely cool, remove from muffin tin. Add a dollop of whipped cream to each tartlet.

Georgia O'Keeffe

Dubbed the mother of American modernism, Presidential Medal of Freedom awardee, painted the record-holder for highest price paid for a work by a female artist

"I've always been absolutely terrified every single moment of my life, and I've never let it stop me from doing a single thing I wanted to do."

Judy Blume

Young adult author, Library of Congress Living Legend, education and intellectual freedom advocate

"My only advice is to stay aware, listen carefully, and yell for help if you need it."

Judy Blumeberry Muffins

BLUEBERRY MUFFINS

SERVING SIZE

Makes 1 to 1½ dozen muffins

INGREDIENTS

2 cups plus 2 teaspoons all-purpose flour, divided

½ cup quick oats

2 teaspoons baking powder

½ teaspoon baking soda

1 teaspoon salt

½ cup unsalted butter, softened (1 stick)

¾ cup granulated sugar

¼ cup brown sugar

2 tablespoons nonfat dry milk

¼ cup honey

1 teaspoon vanilla extract

2 eggs

½ cup whole milk

2 cups blueberries

1. Preheat oven to 375°F and line a 12-well muffin tin with cupcake liners.

2. Sift 2 cups of the flour into a medium mixing bowl. Add oats, baking powder, baking soda, and salt and whisk together. Set aside.

3. In a large mixing bowl, mix butter, granulated sugar, brown sugar, nonfat dry milk, honey, and vanilla extract with an electric mixer on medium speed until creamed, about 3 minutes.

4. Add eggs one at a time, mixing well after each addition and scraping down the sides of the bowl as needed.

5. Add dry ingredients to the wet ingredients ⅓ cup at a time, mixing until combined after each addition. Scrape down the sides of the bowl as needed.

6. Add milk and mix well for 1 minute more.

7. In a small bowl, combine blueberries with the remaining 2 teaspoons flour. Toss blueberries to coat. This will prevent the blueberries from dropping to the bottom of the muffins. Fold floured blueberries gently into the batter until evenly distributed.

8. Pour batter into muffin tin to fill each well about four-fifths full.

9. Bake for 30 to 35 minutes, or until muffins are set and a toothpick comes out clean when inserted.

10. Allow muffins to cool at least 10 minutes in muffin tin, then transfer to cooling rack to finish cooling.

Kathryn Bigelow

First and only female to win the Academy Award for Best Director, producer, and screenwriter

"If there is specific resistance to women making movies, I just to choose to ignore that as an obstacle for two reasons: I can't change my gender and I refuse to stop making movies."

Kathraisin Bigeloaf

CINNAMON RAISIN LOAF

SERVING SIZE
Makes 1 medium loaf

INGREDIENTS

Bread

¾ cup raisins

1 cup whole milk

2 tablespoons granulated sugar

2 teaspoons active dry yeast (one 0.25-ounce packet)

6 tablespoons unsalted butter, melted

2 large eggs

2 ¾ cups all-purpose flour

½ cup whole wheat flour

¼ cup old-fashioned oats

1 teaspoon salt

Cinnamon Filling

2 tablespoons unsalted butter, melted

3 tablespoons brown sugar

2½ tablespoons ground cinnamon

1. **FOR THE BREAD:** Pour raisins into a small bowl and cover with lukewarm water to rehydrate. Set aside.

2. In a small bowl or measuring cup, combine milk, sugar, and yeast and let sit for 5 to 10 minutes, or until mixture starts to lightly foam. This indicates the yeast is alive.

3. Pour yeast mixture into a large mixing bowl and whisk in melted butter and eggs.

4. In a separate large mixing bowl, whisk together all-purpose flour, whole wheat flour, oats, and salt. Add flour mixture to the liquid mixture about 1 cup at a time, kneading with an electric mixer fitted with a dough hook between each addition.

5. Drain and dry raisins and add to the dough. Continue to knead with the dough hook for 10 minutes.

6. Leave dough in bowl, grease the top slightly, cover with a towel or plastic wrap, and let sit for 1 hour, or until the dough about doubles in size.

7. Grease a 9-inch x 5-inch loaf pan and flour a clean countertop or piece of parchment paper. Roll out dough into a 5-inch x 18-inch rectangle.

8. **FOR THE CINNAMON FILLING:** Whisk melted butter, brown sugar, and cinnamon together in a small bowl.

9. Pour filling onto the dough and spread evenly across with a spatula, leaving an inch border on all sides.

10. Roll dough tightly and place in the prepared pan. Cover the loaf pan with plastic wrap or a towel and let sit for 30 minutes to rise.

11. Preheat oven to 375°F and bake bread for 40 to 50 minutes, or until a hard, brown crust forms across the top. Allow bread to cool completely before slicing.

BREADS

Lilly
Pulitzer
Rousseau

*Designer,
American socialite,
entrepreneur, fruit
stand owner*

"Happiness never
goes out of style!"

Lilly Pulinzer Cookies

LINZER COOKIES

SERVING SIZE

Makes 2 to 3 dozen cookie sandwiches

INGREDIENTS

2½ cups all-purpose flour

1 cup almond flour or meal

¼ teaspoon baking powder

¼ teaspoon salt

1 cup unsalted butter, softened (2 sticks)

¾ cup granulated sugar

1 tablespoon lemon zest

1 egg

1 teaspoon vanilla extract

about ½ cup jam of choice

powdered sugar for dusting

1. In a medium bowl, whisk all-purpose flour, almond flour, baking powder, and salt together. Set aside.

2. In a large mixing bowl, mix butter, sugar, and lemon zest together with an electric mixer on medium speed until creamed, about 3 minutes. Add egg and vanilla extract and continue to mix until combined.

3. Add flour mixture and mix until just combined. Be careful to not overmix, or cookies can become tough.

4. Divide dough in half and wrap each piece in plastic wrap. Place in refrigerator to chill for at least 1 hour.

5. When dough has chilled, preheat oven to 350°F and line 2 to 3 baking sheets with parchment paper.

6. Place each piece of dough between 2 pieces of parchment paper and roll out to a thin slab, about ½ inch to ¼ inch thick and cut out cookies with a round cookie cutter about 2 inches in diameter. With a smaller cookie cutter, cut smaller holes or shapes out of the centers of half the cookies.

7. Place cookies on lined baking sheets and bake for 10 minutes, or until bottoms start to brown. Allow cookies to cool completely on a cooling rack.

8. When cool, top each of the cookies without a hole with ½ teaspoon of jam. Sprinkle powdered sugar over the top of the cookies with a hole.

9. Sandwich the cookies with holes, powdered sugar side up, on top of the jam cookies to make sandwich cookies.

COOKIES

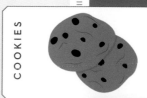

Recommended jam flavors include strawberry, blackberry, apricot, and raspberry. Take your inspiration from a Lilly dress and use jams with bright colors for the best effect.

Maya Angelou

*Writer, poet, Grammy
Award winner,
Presidential
Freedom awardee,
civil rights activist*

"I'm a woman
Phenomenally.
Phenomenal woman,
That's me."

Maya Angelou Caged Hummingbird Cake

HUMMINGBIRD CAKE

SERVING SIZE

Serves about 12

INGREDIENTS

Cake

3¼ cups all-purpose flour

¾ teaspoon baking soda

1½ teaspoons ground cinnamon

½ teaspoon salt

3 eggs

2 cups granulated sugar

2 cups mashed banana

8 ounces canned crushed pineapple, with juice

¾ cup vegetable or canola oil

2 tablespoons rum

1 teaspoon vanilla extract

¾ cup diced pecans

1. Preheat oven to 350°F and grease three 9-inch cake pans.

2. **FOR THE CAKE:** In a medium mixing bowl, whisk together flour, baking soda, cinnamon, and salt.

3. In a large mixing bowl, mix eggs and sugar together with an electric mixer on medium speed until combined. Add mashed banana, crushed pineapple and its juice, oil, rum, and vanilla extract and mix until combined.

4. Add dry ingredients to wet ingredients about 1 cup at a time and mix until combined after each addition. Fold pecans into dough and stir with a wooden spoon or spatula until combined.

5. Divide dough among the 3 cake pans and bake for 25 to 30 minutes, or until a toothpick comes out clean when inserted. Allow cakes to cool for about 30 minutes in pans.

6. **FOR THE FROSTING:** While cakes are cooling, whisk together cream cheese and butter with an electric mixer on medium speed until creamed. Sift in powdered sugar 1 cup at a time, whisking until combined after each addition. Add in vanilla extract and salt and whisk on medium-high speed for about 2 minutes, or until frosting is light and fluffy.

continued →

CAKES & CUPCAKES

155

Frosting

8 ounces cream cheese, softened

½ cup unsalted butter, softened (1 stick)

2½ cups powdered sugar

1 teaspoon vanilla extract

pinch of salt

chopped pecans for garnish, optional

7   Run a knife along the edges of each cake and remove cakes from pans.

8   Flip the first cake upside down and place on a piece of parchment paper or a cake stand. Add a thick layer of frosting and spread it evenly across the top of the cake. Flip the second cake upside down and place on top of the frosted cake. Add another layer of frosting and spread evenly across the top of the second cake. Flip the third cake upside down and place on top of the two cakes.

9   With an offset spatula or knife, spread the remaining frosting over the top and sides of the three-layer cake.

10 Decorate the top and sides of the cake with pecans, if desired.

Nina Garcia
MariÉclairs

ÉCLAIRS

SERVING SIZE

Makes 3 dozen
small éclairs

INGREDIENTS

Pastry Cream
4 egg yolks
¼ cup granulated sugar
2 teaspoons vanilla
extract
⅓ cup cornstarch
⅛ teaspoon salt
2 cups whole milk
2 tablespoons unsalted
butter

Éclairs
½ cup whole milk
½ cup water
½ cup unsalted butter
(1 stick)
2 tablespoons sugar
¼ teaspoon salt
1 cup all-purpose flour
4 eggs

1. **FOR THE PASTRY CREAM:** Whisk together egg yolks, sugar, and vanilla extract in a large mixing bowl with an electric mixer on high speed until doubled in size, about 3 minutes.

2. Sift cornstarch and salt into a small mixing bowl, then whisk into egg mixture 1 tablespoon at a time. Set egg mixture aside.

3. In a medium saucepan, bring milk to a boil, then reduce to medium-low heat. Remove 1 cup of hot liquid and allow to cool for 2 minutes. Slowly whisk the cooled liquid into the egg-and-sugar mixture until combined. Pour this mixture back into the saucepan.

4. Bring mixture back to a boil over medium heat, whisking constantly, until mixture thickens into a pudding-like texture. This can take between 2 and 5 minutes.

5. Remove from heat and pour into a medium bowl. (If small, clear lumps of cornstarch have formed, pour mixture through a wire mesh strainer into the bowl.) Gently fold in butter and mix very gently until butter is melted and combined.

6. Cover pastry cream with plastic wrap placed on the surface of the cream. Refrigerate until cool.

7. Preheat oven to 400°F and line 2 to 3 baking sheets with parchment paper.

continued →

TRADITIONAL DESSERTS

Chocolate Sauce

⅓ cup heavy whipping cream

½ cup semisweet chocolate chips (4 ounces)

8   **FOR THE ÉCLAIRS:** Whisk together milk, water, butter, sugar, and salt in a medium saucepan and bring to a low boil over medium heat.

9   Pour flour directly into simmering liquid and mix with a heat-resistant spatula or wooden spoon until dough comes together in a smooth ball, 1 to 2 minutes.

10   Transfer dough to a large mixing bowl and allow to cool slightly, about 5 minutes, or until steam is no longer released when mixed. When dough has cooled slightly, beat in eggs, one at a time, with an electric mixer on a medium-low speed until fully incorporated.

11   Transfer dough to a large piping bag with a 1-inch tip, or transfer to a plastic gallon storage bag and cut one corner to create a 1-inch hole. Pipe 3-to-4-inch-long logs onto parchment paper. Push any points of dough back down into logs with a wet finger to prevent them from burning.

12   Bake éclairs for 17 to 22 minutes, or until they start to turn golden. Remove from oven and puncture a hole on each end of each éclair with a large toothpick or chopstick to release steam. You will pipe the pastry cream into these holes. Transfer éclairs to a cooling rack and allow to cool completely.

13   Transfer pastry cream to a piping bag with a very small tip, about ⅛ inch, or transfer to a plastic storage bag and cut one corner to create an ⅛-inch hole. Pipe pastry cream into the hole on either end of each éclair. Alternatively, cut éclairs in half and pipe pastry cream in the center.

14   **FOR THE CHOCOLATE SAUCE:** Heat heavy cream in a microwave-safe bowl for about 45 seconds, or until just about simmering. Place chocolate in a medium bowl. Pour cream over chocolate and allow to sit for about 1 minute, or until chocolate looks soft. Whisk cream and chocolate together until smooth and shiny.

15   Dip each éclair into chocolate mixture and set on cooling rack to allow chocolate to set.

Pastry cream can be made up to 3 days in advance and stored in the refrigerator.

Nina Garcia

First Latin editor-in-chief of a major fashion magazine, fashion director, author, reality television judge

"Confidence is captivating, it is powerful, and it does not fade—and that is endlessly more interesting than beauty."

Nora Ephron

Author, journalist, director, Academy Award–nominated screenwriter, Tony Award–nominated playwright

"Above all, be the heroine of your life, not the victim."

Nora Ephron Heartburn Brownies

SPICY CHOCOLATE BROWNIES

SERVING SIZE

Makes 1½ to 2 dozen brownies

INGREDIENTS

1 cup all-purpose flour

1 teaspoon ground cinnamon

¼ teaspoon ground cayenne pepper

¾ cup dark chocolate squares (6 ounces)

¾ cup unsalted butter (1½ sticks)

2 cups granulated sugar

3 eggs

2 tablespoons honey

1 teaspoon vanilla extract

1. Preheat oven to 350°F and grease an 9-inch x 13-inch baking dish.

2. In a medium mixing bowl, whisk together flour, cinnamon, and cayenne and set aside

3. Melt chocolate and butter in a large microwave-safe bowl in 45-second intervals, stirring between each interval, or in a double boiler over medium-low heat while stirring constantly. Stir until smooth and remove from heat.

4. Add sugar to the melted chocolate mixture and mix until combined. The sugar will not completely dissolve in the chocolate and will remain grainy.

5. Add eggs, honey, and vanilla extract and mix by hand with a wooden spoon or with an electric mixer on low speed until combined.

6. Slowly add the flour mixture about ⅓ cup at a time, mixing on low speed or by hand until fully incorporated between each addition.

7. Pour batter into prepared baking dish and bake for 30 to 35 minutes, or until the middle is set and a toothpick comes out clean when inserted. Allow to cool completely before cutting into squares.

BROWNIES & BARS

Iris Apfel

*Interior designer,
design restorer for
the White House,
businesswoman,
fashion icon*

"I don't have any rules
because I would only
be breaking them."

Pieris Apfel Crust

FLOUR PIE CRUST

SERVING SIZE

Makes two 9-inch to 10-inch pie crusts

INGREDIENTS

2 cups all-purpose flour

1½ tablespoons sugar

1 teaspoon salt

12 tablespoons unsalted butter

¼ cup cold water

1. In a large mixing bowl, whisk flour, sugar, and salt together for about 1 minute to aerate the flour and ensure there are no lumps.

2. Cut butter into ¼-inch cubes and cut into flour mixture 2 tablespoons at a time. Work into dough using a fork, your hands, or an electric mixer fitted with the whisk attachment at medium speed. Dough should be an even crumbled texture, and large chunks of butter should be broken down. Smaller, pea-sized chunks of butter are okay, as they will be broken down later in the process.

3. Add water 1 tablesoon at a time, and fold into dough with a spatula or wooden spoon. As dough comes together, knead into a loose ball.

4. Transfer dough to a piece of floured parchment paper. Cut dough into 2 equal pieces and roll each piece into a thick disk about 6 inches in diameter. Wrap in plastic wrap and refrigerate for at least 30 minutes. Dough can be stored up to 1 week in the refrigerator.

5. Allow dough to sit at room temperature for 5 minutes before rolling out to desired shape and baking according to your recipe.

How To Bake Your Crust

A pie crust will be baked differently depending on the type of filling that is going into the crust. If you are baking a recipe from this cookbook, crust-baking instructions will be included in that recipe. If you are using this crust for a different recipe or creating a new recipe, it is generally a good idea to anchor your crust down to your pie pan by stabbing the bottom with a fork, covering it with parchment, and weighing it down with baking beans. Crust can then be baked at 400°F for 20 to 25 minutes, until the middle is soft but edges begin to brown, before adding filling.

Zelda
Fitzgerald

*Dubbed the first
American flapper,
American socialite,
novelist, painter*

———————

"She refused to be
bored chiefly because
she wasn't boring."

Pretzelda Fitzgerald

SOFT PRETZELS

Makes 1 dozen pretzels

INGREDIENTS

Pretzels

2¼ teaspoons active
dry yeast (one
0.25-ounce
packet)

2 teaspoons granulated
sugar

1 cup warm water

½ cup whole milk

1 tablespoon unsalted
butter, melted

¼ cup dark brown sugar

4 cups bread flour

2 teaspoons salt

Water Bath

8 cups water

¼ cup baking soda

Topping

1 tablespoon sea salt

2 tablespoons unsalted
butter, melted

1   **FOR THE PRETZELS:** In a large mixing bowl, whisk yeast, granulated sugar, and warm water together. Let sit for 5 to 10 minutes, or until mixture has a light foam on the surface. This indicates the yeast is alive.

2   Whisk milk, melted butter, and brown sugar into mixture with an electric mixer on medium-low speed until combined.

3   Whisk in 2 cups of the bread flour and salt. Change mixing attachment to a dough hook and add the remaining 2 cups of flour. Knead on medium speed until the dough forms a ball, then continue to knead for an 2 additional minutes.

4   Transfer dough to a greased bowl and grease the top of the dough. Cover with plastic wrap and allow to sit for 30 minutes to 1 hour, until the dough about doubles in size.

5   Preheat oven to 450°F and line 2 to 3 baking sheets with parchment paper. Grease the parchment paper.

6   **FOR THE WATER BATH:** In a large saucepan, bring 8 cups of water to a simmer. Add baking soda and whisk until combined. Bring water back to a simmer.

continued →

BREADS

7   When dough is ready, cut dough into 12 even sections. Roll each piece out into a 16-inch to 20-inch-long rope. Twist dough into a pretzel shape by shaping it into a U, crossing over the ends, twisting, then sealing each end to the bottom of pretzel.

8   Allow dough to rest for about 5 minutes, then drop pretzels one by one into simmering water for 15 to 20 seconds. Remove pretzels with a slotted spoon and place onto prepared baking sheets.

9   **FOR THE TOPPING:** Sprinkle pretzels with sea salt and bake for 15 minutes, or until golden brown.

10 Remove from oven and immediatley brush baked pretzels with butter.

11 Pretzels are best enjoyed the same day they are baked.

To make pretzel bites, cut the dough into small balls, drop into the water bath for 5 to 10 seconds, and bake for 8 to 10 minutes.

Zaha Hadid Blueprintstachio Tart

PISTACHIO DARK CHOCOLATE TART

SERVING SIZE
Serves 8 to 10

INGREDIENTS

Crust
½ cup pistachios, toasted
1 cup all-purpose flour
¼ cup granulated sugar
5 tablespoons unsalted butter, melted
2 tablespoons whole milk

Pistachio Butter
¼ cup pistachios, toasted
1 tablespoon agave syrup
1½ teaspoons vegetable or other neutral oil

Filling
½ cup dark chocolate squares (4 ounces)
⅓ cup heavy cream
crushed pistachios, optional

1. Preheat oven to 350°F and grease a 9-inch tart pan with a removable bottom.

2. **FOR THE CRUST:** Pulse pistachios in a food processor for 20 to 30 seconds to create crumbs. Transfer to a large mixing bowl.

3. Add flour and sugar to mixing bowl and whisk together. Slowly add melted butter about 1 tablespoon at a time, and mix with an electric mixer on low speed or by hand with a wooden spoon until the mixture becomes crumbly.

4. Add milk and mix until combined.

5. Press crust into tart pan and up onto the sides. Cover crust with parchment paper and place baking beans, baking weights, or rice onto parchment. Bake crust for 25 minutes, or until set.

6. **FOR THE PISTACHIO BUTTER:** In a food processor, combine pistachios, agave syrup, and oil. Pulse until a peanut butter–like mixture forms, about 5 minutes, stopping to scrape down the sides of the bowl as needed. Transfer mixture to a piping bag, or transfer to a plastic gallon storage bag and cut one corner to create a ½-inch hole, and set aside.

continued →

167

7   FOR THE FILLING: Place dark chocolate in a medium mixing bowl. Set aside.

8   Heat cream in a saucepan over low heat, or in the microwave in 45-second intervals, until it starts to simmer on the sides. Pour hot cream over chocolate and let sit for 1 minute, or until chocolate looks softened.

9   Stir cream and chocolate together until chocolate is completely melted and the mixture is smooth and shiny.

10 Pour dark chocolate onto tart crust and spread evenly with a spatula. Pipe pistachio butter on top of dark chocolate in a swirl or design of your choice.

11 Sprinkle crushed pistachios in center or along edges, if desired.

12 Place tart in the refrigerator and allow to chill for at least 1 hour before serving.

If a sweeter chocolate center is desired, substitute milk chocolate for the dark chocolate.

Zaha Hadid

Multi-award-winning architect, first female to win the Pritzker Prize, advocate for women in the creative fields

"Yes, I'm a feminist, because I see all women as smart, gifted, and tough."

Athletes

Female athletes not only have to dedicate hard work and determination in order to be the best in their sport, they also have to do so without equal recognition or pay compared with their male counterparts. Kathrine Switzer defiantly ran the men's-only Boston Marathon ten years before Nike even made the world's first women's running shoe. Billie Jean King heroically petitioned for equal pay in tennis, and took on professional male tennis player Bobby Riggs to prove women were as talented and capable as men in the sport. Mia Hamm's iconic "anything you can do, I can do better" Gatorade commercial with Michael Jordan inspired young girls all over the country to believe that they, too, could compete with the boys. These women are more than just top *female* athletes; they are top athletes.

Billie Jean King

Founder of the Women's Tennis Association, advocate for gender equality, Presidential Medal of Freedom awardee

"Ever since that day when I was eleven years old, and I wasn't allowed in a photo because I wasn't wearing a tennis skirt, I knew that I wanted to change the sport."

Billie Jean King Cake

KING CAKE

SERVING SIZE
Serves 15 to 20

INGREDIENTS

Brioche Cake

3¾ cups all-purpose flour

⅓ cup granulated sugar

2¼ teaspoons active dry yeast (one 0.25-ounces packet)

1¼ teaspoons salt

10 tablespoons unsalted butter, melted

⅔ cup whole milk

2 eggs

2 egg yolks

Filling

4 ounces cream cheese, softened

¼ cup light brown sugar

1 teaspoon ground cinnamon

1 teaspoon vanilla extract

1. **FOR THE BRIOCHE CAKE:** In a large mixing bowl, whisk flour, sugar, yeast, and salt together until combined.

2. Add melted butter and milk and knead with an electric mixer fitted with the dough hook attachment, stopping to scrape down the sides and bottom of the bowl as needed to incorporate all the flour.

3. Add eggs and egg yolks and continue to knead for 5 to 8 minutes, or until a soft and sticky dough forms that pulls away from the sides and can be worked into a ball. If dough is too sticky to handle with hands, add additional flour 1 tablespoon at a time, but ensure dough still remains sticky.

4. Transfer dough to a separate mixing bowl and cover with a towel or plastic wrap. Set in the refrigerator to rest for 1 hour.

5. **FOR THE FILLING:** While dough is resting, beat cream cheese in a medium mixing bowl with an electric mixer on medium-high speed until fluffy, about 1 minute. Add brown sugar, cinnamon, and vanilla extract and mix on medim speed until combined.

6. Transfer dough to a lightly floured surface. Knead the dough a few times by hand to ensure it is elastic, then work it back into a ball. Lightly flour the dough and a rolling pin.

7. Roll dough into a 20-inch x 12-inch rectangle. Spread cream cheese filling across one half of the long end (making a 20-inch x 6-inch rectangle of filling). Fold the uncovered dough over onto the covered half like a book and pat down firmly.

continued →

CAKES & CUPCAKES

173

Topping

2 cups powdered sugar

2 tablespoons milk (dairy or non-dairy)

½ teaspoon vanilla extract

purple, green, and yellow sprinkles

8   Cut the dough parallel to the long side into three 2-inch-wide strips. Press the top ends together and braid the strips. If you are uncomfortable with braiding, dough can also be cut into 2 strips and twisted together. Seal any parts of the dough that have broken and have filling oozing out.

9   Stretch the braid so that it is 20 inches long again and shape into a circle. Transfer to a large baking sheet lined with parchment paper, cover with plastic wrap, and let rise for 1 hour. Dough should become puffy and about double in size.

10   Preheat oven to 350°F. When dough has risen, bake for 35 to 40 minutes, or until cake is golden on the top and bottom.

11   **FOR THE TOPPING:** While brioche is cooling, make the glaze by sifting powdered sugar into a medium bowl. Whisk in milk and vanilla extract by hand or with an electric mixer at low speed until a thin glaze forms. If glaze is too thick, add additional milk 1 teaspoon at a time.

12   When king cake is completely cool, spoon icing over the cake and cover with alternating sections of purple, green, and yellow sprinkles. We recommend icing and sprinkling one small section at a time, so the icing does not harden as you work your way around sprinkling the cake.

Traditional king cakes are very large because they are meant to serve an entire party, and this recipe is no exception. If you prefer, you can halve the recipe to make a standard cake size. If halving the cake, make a 12-inch x 8-inch rectangle in step 7. Size may reduce bake time by 5 to 10 minutes.

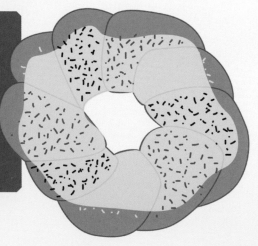

Kathrine Switzer Boston Marathon Cream Poke Cake

BOSTON CREAM POKE CAKE

SERVING SIZE
Serves 12 to 15

INGREDIENTS

Pastry Cream
2 egg yolks
2 tablespoons granulated sugar
1 teaspoon vanilla extract
1 tablespoon cornstarch
⅛ teaspoon salt
1½ cups whole milk
1 tablespoon unsalted butter

1. **FOR THE PASTRY CREAM:** In a large mixing bowl, whisk egg yolks, sugar, and vanilla extract together with an electric mixer on high speed until doubled in size, about 3 minutes.

2. Sift cornstarch and salt into a small bowl and whisk into egg mixture. Set aside.

3. In a medium saucepan, bring milk to a boil, then reduce to medium-low heat. Remove 1 cup of hot liquid and allow to cool for 2 minutes. Slowly whisk the cooled liquid into the egg-and-sugar mixture until combined. Pour this mixture back into the saucepan.

4. Over medium heat, bring the mixture back to a boil and whisk constantly until it thickens to a thin, pudding-like texture. This can take between 2 and 5 minutes.

5. Remove from heat and pour into a medium bowl. (If small, clear lumps of cornstarch have formed, pour mixture through a wire mesh strainer into the bowl.) Gently fold in butter and mix very gently until butter is melted and combined.

6. Cover pastry cream with plastic wrap placed on the surface of the cream. Refrigerate while cake is baking.

CAKES & CUPCAKES

continued →

Cake

1¾ cups all-purpose flour

2 teaspoons baking powder

1 teaspoon salt

3 eggs

1 egg yolk

1½ cups granulated sugar

¾ cup whole milk

6 tablespoons unsalted butter

Chocolate Ganache

½ cup semisweet chocolate chips (4 ounces)

⅓ cup heavy cream

1 tablespoon corn syrup

> Pastry cream can be made up to 3 days in advance and stored in the refrigerator.

7   **FOR THE CAKE:** Preheat oven to 350°F and grease a 10-inch x 15-inch pan completely, including sides.

8   Sift flour, baking powder, and salt together in a medium bowl. Set aside.

9   In a large mixing bowl whisk together eggs, egg yolk, and sugar with an electric mixer on high speed for 2 to 3 minutes, or until mixture is light and airy. The air incorporated into the mixture is important to achieve a light and fluffy cake texture.

10 Add flour mixture to the batter ½ cup at a time, mixing until combined between each addition.

11 In a small saucepan or microwave-safe bowl, heat milk and butter until butter is completely melted. Stir until combined. Slowly pour milk mixture into batter and mix until combined.

12 Pour batter into prepared pan and bake for 25 to 30 minutes, or until cake is set and a toothpick comes out clean when inserted.

13 Allow cake to cool slightly, about 15 minutes. With a thick straw or the handle end of a wooden spoon or spatula, poke about sixty ½-inch holes into the cake, about 6 down and 10 across.

14 Pour cooled pastry cream onto cake and spread to cover all the holes. Some pastry cream will remain on top of the cake.

15 Place cake in the refrigerator and allow to cool for 2 hours.

16 **FOR THE CHOCOLATE GANACHE:** Place chocolate in a heatproof bowl. Heat heavy cream and corn syrup in a saucepan at medium heat until just beginning to simmer, or in the microwave for 45 seconds. Pour cream over the chocolate and allow to sit for about 1 minute. When chocolate looks soft, whisk or stir the chocolate into the cream until smooth. If needed, return to the microwave for an additional 10 seconds.

17 Pour chocolate on top of cake and spread evenly. Chill cake in the refrigerator for an additional hour to allow chocolate to set before serving.

Kathrine Switzer

First woman to run the Boston Marathon as a numbered entrant, New York Marathon winner, Emmy Award–winning TV commentator, women's empowerment advocate

"Life is for participating, not for spectating."

261

Lisa Leslie

Professional basketball player, four-time Olympic gold medalist, first player to dunk in a WNBA game, model

"Be at peace with your femininity and throwing elbows."

Lisa Leslie Dunked Doughnuts

OLD-FASHIONED DOUGHNUTS

continued →

SERVING SIZE

Makes 1 to 1½ dozen doughnuts

INGREDIENTS

Doughnuts

2 cups bread flour

1¾ cups all-purpose flour

⅓ cup granulated sugar

2 teaspoons baking powder

½ teaspoon salt

1 cup whole milk, warm

1 egg

3 tablespoons unsalted butter, melted

½ teaspoon vanilla extract

2¼ teaspoons active dry yeast (one 0.25-ounce packet)

oil for frying

1. **FOR THE DOUGHNUTS:** In a medium mixing bowl, whisk together bread flour, all-purpose flour, sugar, baking powder, and salt. Set aside.

2. In a large mixing bowl, whisk together milk, egg, butter, vanilla extract, and yeast with an electric mixer on medium-low speed until combined.

3. Change mixing attachment to a dough hook. Add dry ingredients to wet ingredients and knead with an electric mixer on medium speed for about 5 minutes, or until a smooth dough forms.

4. Place dough in a greased bowl and gently grease the top of the dough. Cover with plastic wrap or a cloth and let sit for 1 to 2 hours, or until dough doubles in size.

5. Remove dough from bowl and knead with hands for about 1 minute Roll out dough into a rough rectangle that is ¼ to ½ inch thick. Cut doughnuts with a doughnut cutter, or cut circles with a 2½-to-3-inch cookie cutter and then cut holes out of the middle with a ½-inch cookie cutter.

BREAKFAST SWEETS

Glaze

2 cups powdered sugar

3 to 4 tablespoons milk (dairy or non-dairy)

1 teaspoon vanilla extract

⅛ teaspoon salt

6   Place doughnuts on a greased baking sheet and cover with plastic wrap. Let sit for 30 minutes, until doubled in size, or in the refrigerator overnight. (If resting dough overnight, remove it from the refrigerator 1 hour before frying and let sit until dough comes back to room temperature and is puffy.)

7   **FOR THE GLAZE:** Sift powdered sugar into a medium mixing bowl and whisk in milk, vanilla extract, and salt until a thin glaze forms. Add additional milk 1 teaspoon at a time if needed. Set aside.

8   Fill a large pot with at least 4 inches of oil. Heat oil to 350°F. Working in batches, drop doughnuts into hot oil and fry for 1 to 2 minutes on each side, or until golden brown.

9   Place fried doughnuts on a paper towel on a cooling rack or in paper bags to remove excess oil. Dunk in glaze and set on a separate drying rack with parchment paper or a baking sheet underneath to catch excess glaze.

10 Serve warm with a cup of coffee.

Mia Hamm & Cheese Foldovers

HAM-AND-CHEESE FOLDOVER CROISSANTS

SERVING SIZE

Makes 6 foldovers

INGREDIENTS

Puff Pastry

2 cups chilled all-purpose flour

½ teaspoon salt

12 tablespoons cold unsalted butter, divided

½ cup cold water

Foldovers

2 tablespoons Dijon mustard

½ cup grated gruyere cheese

6 thick slices ham

1 egg, beaten

1 tablespoon poppy seeds

1. **FOR THE PUFF PASTRY:** If possible, place flour in the refrigerator overnight prior to beginning recipe in order to keep the dough as cold as possible throughout the process.

2. In a medium mixing bowl, whisk together chilled flour and salt.

3. Dice 10 tablespoons of the cold butter into ¼-inch cubes. Cut butter into the flour mixture with a pastry cutter, a fork, or your hands until the mixture is crumbly and even. Small, pea-sized chunks of butter can remain, as they will be worked in later in the process.

4. Slowly pour ½ cup cold water into flour mixture and work in with your hands or a spatula until dough starts to come together in a ball. If dough does not come together, stick in the refrigerator for 5 minutes to chill.

5. Transfer dough to a lightly floured work surface and roll out into a long rectangle, about 12-inches x 4-inches. Fold one of the short ends in about a third of the way, then fold the opposite short end over the top, like folding a paper for an envelope, so that you have a 3-inch x 4-inch rectangle with 3 layers.

continued →

BREADS

6 Rotate the dough 90 degrees and roll out to another 12-inch x 4-inch rectangle. Fold once again into 3 layers and rotate 90 degrees. Repeat this process a total of 3 times. Cover the top of the 12-inch x 4-inch rectangle with 1 tablespoon of cold butter cut into slices.

7 Repeat the folding process 2 more times, then cover the top of the 12-inch x 4-inch rectangle with the remaining 1 tablespoon cold butter cut into slices. Fold a sixth and final time. The folds create the flaky layers in the puff pastry when it is baked. If dough becomes too soft and sticky during the process, cover it with plastic wrap and place in the refrigerator for 15 minutes to chill.

8 When dough has been folded and turned 6 times, cover in plastic wrap and transfer to the refrigerator for 30 minutes to chill.

9 **FOR THE FOLDOVERS:** Preheat oven to 450°F and line 1 to 2 baking sheets with parchment paper.

10 Roll dough into a 15-inch x 12-inch rectangle, then cut into six 5-inch x 6-inch rectangles.

11 Spread 1 teaspoon Dijon mustard onto each rectangle. Add a heaping tablespoon of grated cheese on top of each rectangle.

12 Place 1 slice of thick ham diagonally across the rectangle and fold ends of ham into the center.

13 Take two opposite ends of each rectangle and fold into the center. Brush folded ends with the beaten egg and sprinkle with poppy seeds. Press down the top end firmly to seal.

14 Place foldovers onto prepared baking sheet and bake for 30 to 35 minutes, or until tops and bottoms are golden brown.

15 Allow foldovers to cool about 5 minutes on baking sheets before serving.

If you would prefer to use frozen store-bought puff pastry, thaw it first and start preparation at step 8.

Mia Hamm

Five-time US female soccer athlete of the year, two-time Olympic gold medalist, first woman inducted into the World Football Hall of Fame

"My coach said I run like a girl, and I said if he ran a little faster, he could too."

Misty May-Treanor and Kerri Walsh Jennings

Beach volleyball athletes, teammates of twelve years, undefeated three-time Olympic gold medalists

"This was so much more about the friendship, the togetherness, the journey—and volleyball was just a small part of it."
—Misty May-Treanor

Misty Maple & Kerri Waffles

MAPLE WAFFLES

SERVING SIZE

Makes about 6 large waffles

INGREDIENTS

1½ cups all-purpose flour

2 tablespoons cornstarch

1 tablespoon baking powder

½ teaspoon salt

2 tablespoons sugar

1½ cups buttermilk

½ cup maple syrup

2 eggs

6 tablespoons unsalted butter, melted

1½ teaspoons maple extract

¼ cup cooked bacon bits, optional

1. Heat or turn on waffle maker and grease if needed.

2. In a medium mixing bowl, whisk together flour, cornstarch, baking powder, and salt. Set aside.

3. In a large mixing bowl, mix sugar, buttermilk, maple syrup, eggs, melted butter, and maple extract until combined.

4. With a spatula or wooden spoon, gently mix dry ingredients into wet ingredients until just combined. Be careful to not overmix.

5. If desired, fold bacon bits into batter.

6. Transfer about ½ cup of batter to a large measuring cup. Pour batter into waffle maker and cook until steam is no longer released from waffle maker, about 3 to 5 minutes.

7. Repeat with the remaining batter, greasing the waffle maker between waffles as needed. Serve warm with butter and additional maple syrup, or with powdered sugar, if desired.

To make waffles extra crispy, transfer warm waffles to a 250°F oven for 5 minutes.

Kristi Yamaguchi

American professional figure skater, Olympic gold medalist, US Olympic Hall of Fame inductee

"An athlete gains so much knowledge by just participating in a sport. Focus, discipline, hard work, goal setting and, of course, the thrill of finally achieving those goals. These are all lessons in life."

Rice Kristi Yamaguchi

COCONUT MARSHMALLOW RICE TREATS

SERVING SIZE

Makes about 2 dozen treats

INGREDIENTS

5½ cups rice cereal

¾ cups shredded sweetened coconut

¼ cup unrefined coconut oil

10 ounces mini marshmallows

½ cup white chocolate melting wafers (4 ounces)

¼ cup sprinkles, optional

1. Grease a 9-inch x 13-inch baking dish and a spatula with butter or non-stick spray.

2. In a medium mixing bowl, combine rice cereal and shredded coconut and mix until evenly distributed.

3. In a large microwave-safe mixing bowl, combine coconut oil and marshmallows and microwave for 2 minutes. Mix with greased spatula. Return to microwave for 1 additional minute.

4. Add cereal mixture to marshmallows 1 cup at a time, mixing with greased spatula until combined after each addition.

5. Pour mixture into greased baking pan and press evenly into the pan with greased spatula or greased hands.

6. Melt white melting chocolate in the microwave in 30-second intervals, stirring between each interval, or in a double boiler over low heat, stirring constantly.

7. Transfer chocolate to a piping bag with a ½-inch tip, or transfer to a plastic gallon storage bag and cut one corner to create a ½-inch hole. Pipe white chocolate in zigzags onto marshmallow rice treats and top with sprinkles, if desired.

8. When treats are cool, cut into 2 dozen squares.

> You can also pipe on the white chocolate and add the sprinkles after cutting the treats, if you prefer, for more consistent coverage and pattern.

Venus & Serena Williams

Sisters, professional tennis players, philanthropists, winners of a combined forty-eight grand slam titles, Olympic gold medalists

"I prefer the word 'one of the greatest athletes of all time.'" —Serena Williams, in response to being called "one of the greatest female athletes of all time."

Venus & Serena Doubles Chocolate Cookies

CHOCOLATE CHIP CHOCOLATE COOKIE

SERVING SIZE

Makes 1½ to 2 dozen cookies

INGREDIENTS

2 ⅓ cups all-purpose flour

¾ cup cocoa powder

1 teaspoon baking soda

½ teaspoon salt

1 cup unsalted butter, melted (2 sticks)

¾ cup plus 1 tablespoon granulated sugar, divided

¾ cup brown sugar

1 tablespoon instant coffee grounds

1 teaspoon vanilla extract

2 large eggs

2 cups semisweet mini chocolate chips (16 ounces)

1 Preheat oven to 350°F.

2 In a medium mixing bowl, whisk together flour, cocoa powder, baking soda, and salt and set aside.

3 In a large mixing bowl, mix melted butter, ¾ cup of the granulated sugar, brown sugar, instant coffee, and vanilla extract together with an electric mixer on medium speed until creamed, about 3 minutes.

4 Add eggs one at a time, mixing on a medium speed until combined after each addition.

5 Add dry mixture to wet ingredients about ¾ cup at a time, mixing on medium speed until combined after each addition.

6 Fold chocolate chips into dough and mix with a wooden spoon or spatula until evenly distributed.

7 Drop dough by rounded tablespoons about 4 inches apart onto ungreased baking sheets and sprinkle the remaining 1 tablespoon granulated sugar over unbaked cookies.

8 Bake for 12 to 14 minutes, or until cookies' centers are set.

COOKIES

Michelle Wie

American professional golfer, youngest player to Monday qualify for an LGPA tour, one of six women to play in a men's PGA event

"I don't mind it when I hit a ball into the woods. I think of it as an adventure. That's when golf really gets exciting and interesting."

Michelle Wie Doughnut Holes in One

PUMPKIN DOUGHNUT HOLES

SERVING SIZE

Makes 2 to 2½ dozen doughnut holes

INGREDIENTS

Doughnuts

1 cup all-purpose flour

½ cup whole wheat flour

2 teaspoons baking powder

1 teaspoon pumpkin spice

¼ teaspoon salt

¾ cup pumpkin puree or canned pumpkin

½ cup granulated sugar

4 tablespoons unsalted butter, melted

2 eggs

1 teaspoon vanilla extract

2 tablespoons whole milk

1. Preheat oven to 350°F and grease two 12-well mini muffin tins.

2. **FOR THE DOUGHNUTS:** In a medium mixing bowl, whisk together all-purpose flour, whole wheat flour, baking powder, pumpkin spice, and salt. Set aside.

3. In a large mixing bowl, mix pumpkin puree, sugar, and melted butter with an electric mixer on medium speed until loosely combined.

4. Mix in eggs and vanilla extract until combined.

5. Add flour mixture to pumpkin mixture and mix on medium speed until combined.

6. Add milk and mix until combined.

7. Scoop batter into mini muffin tins until each well is about three-quarters full.

8. Bake doughnut holes for 12 to 15 minutes, or until a toothpick comes out clean when inserted.

continued →

Cinnamon-Sugar Coating

3 tablespoons unsalted butter

½ cup granulated sugar

1 teaspoon ground cinnamon

½ teaspoon pumpkin spice

9   **FOR THE CINNAMON-SUGAR COATING:** While doughnuts are cooling, melt butter in a small bowl and set aside. In a separate small bowl, combine sugar, cinnamon, and pumpkin spice.

10 When doughnuts are cool enough to handle, about 10 minutes, dunk each doughnut hole into the melted butter and roll in cinnamon-sugar mixture to coat.

Pop
Culture
Icons

Pop culture icons have inspired us by openly sharing their vulnerability and strength through their characters, songs, and humor. Women are so often underrepresented and underestimated in the entertainment industry, but icons like Lucille Ball, Whoopi Goldberg, and Cher have proven that women are funny, talented, and versatile. When women like Reese Witherspoon champion making media more inclusive and representative, they empower others to be bold and express themselves through creativity.

Beyoncé Knowles

Singer, songwriter, actor, businesswoman, most nominated woman in Grammy history

"I don't like to gamble, but if there is one thing I'm willing to bet on it's myself."

BeyHive Honey Cake

HONEY ALMOND BUNDT CAKE

SERVING SIZE

Serves 10 to 12

INGREDIENTS

Cake

1 cup sliced almonds, divided

2 cups all-purpose flour

1 teaspoon baking soda

½ teaspoon salt

12 tablespoons unsalted butter, softened

½ cup brown sugar

4 eggs

½ cup honey

⅓ cup plain full-fat yogurt

Glaze

1 cup powdered sugar

2 tablespoons honey

2 tablespoons milk (dairy or non-dairy)

1. Preheat oven to 350°F and grease a 12-cup Bundt cake pan, including sides.

2. **FOR THE CAKE:** Evenly distribute ¾ cup of the almonds across the bottom of the pan and push almonds up onto sides slightly.

3. Sift flour, baking soda, and salt into a medium mixing bowl and set aside.

4. In large mixing bowl, mix butter and brown sugar together with an electric mixer on high speed until fluffy, about 3 minutes.

5. Mix in eggs and honey until combined, scraping down the sides of the bowl as needed.

6. Add flour mixture about ½ cup at a time and mix until combined after each addition.

7. Add yogurt and remaining ¼ cup almonds and mix until combined.

8. Pour batter into Bundt pan and bake for 40 to 45 minutes, or until a toothpick comes out clean when inserted.

9. Allow cake to cool in the Bundt pan completely, then place a cooling rack on top of the pan and invert together to remove the cake from the pan.

10. **FOR THE GLAZE:** While cake is cooling, sift powdered sugar into a clean mixing bowl, then whisk in honey and milk until a thin glaze forms. If glaze is too thick, add additional milk 1 teaspoon at a time.

11. Once cake has cooled, transfer cake on its cooling rack to a baking sheet lined with parchment paper. Pour glaze over cake, allowing it to drip down the sides.

197

Carrie
Fisher

*Actor, author, Disney
Legend, mental health
awareness advocate,
Grammy Award winner*

———————

"Even in space there's
a double standard for
women."

Carrie Fisher Cinnamon Buns

OVERNIGHT CINNAMON ROLLS

SERVING SIZE

Makes 12 cinnamon rolls

INGREDIENTS

Rolls

⅔ cup whole milk, warm

2¼ teaspoons active dry yeast (one 0.25-ounce packet)

2 eggs

2 egg yolks

½ cup unsalted butter, melted (1 stick)

⅓ cup granulated sugar

1½ teaspoons salt

4 cups all-purpose flour

1. **FOR THE ROLLS:** In a small bowl or liquid measuring cup, combine warm milk and yeast. Allow to sit for 10 minutes, or until yeast starts to foam slightly. This indicates the yeast is alive.

2. In a large mixing bowl, whisk together milk mixture, eggs, egg yolks, butter, sugar, and salt with an electric mixer on medium speed for about 1 minute. The mixture will be thin and loosely combined.

3. Whisk in 2 cups of the flour until combined. Change mixing attachment to a dough hook and add the remaining 2 cups of flour. Knead on medium speed for 5 minutes, or until the dough is in a moist, firm ball that is not sticking to the sides of the bowl or your hands.

4. Transfer dough ball to a slightly greased bowl and push down to remove any air pockets. Very lightly grease or oil the top of the dough. Cover the bowl with plastic wrap or a towel and let sit for 2 hours at room temperature, or until dough about doubles in size.

continued →

BREAKFAST SWEETS

Filling

¾ cup brown sugar

1 tablespoon ground cinnamon

3 tablespoons unsalted butter

Icing

2 cups powdered sugar

4 tablespoons unsalted butter, softened

1 teaspoon vanilla extract

2 to 3 tablespoons milk (dairy or non-dairy)

5   **FOR THE FILLING:** In a small mixing bowl, mix together brown sugar and cinnamon. In a separate bowl, melt butter.

6   When dough has risen, lightly grease a 9-inch x 13-inch baking dish and set aside.

7   Transfer dough to a lightly floured surface. Roll out to a 12-inch x 18-inch rectangle. Brush dough with melted butter and sprinkle generously with brown sugar mixture, leaving about an inch uncovered on each long side.

8   Tightly roll the long end up until you have an 18-inch-long cylinder and squeeze the dough along the seam to seal it closed.

9   With a serrated knife, cut cylinder into 1½-inch rolls and arrange them in the baking dish; they should fit 3 rolls by 4 rolls across. Cover with plastic wrap and place in the refrigerator overnight.

10 Before baking, remove rolls from refrigerator and allow to sit at room temperature for 1 hour or in a 100°F oven for 30 minutes. The cinnamon rolls will become large and puffy.

11 When ready to bake, preheat oven to 350°F.

12 Bake rolls for 30 to 35 minutes, or until tops are firm and golden.

13 **FOR THE ICING:** While rolls are baking, sift 1 cup of the powdered sugar into a medium mixing bowl, then whisk in butter and vanilla extract by hand or with an electric mixer on low speed until combined. Add 1 tablespoon milk and continue to whisk. Sift in remaining 1 cup of powdered sugar and whisk until combined, and then add the remaining milk, 1 tablespoon at a time, until desired texture is reached.

14 Allow rolls to cool for 3 to 5 minutes in the pan, then spread icing evenly across rolls. Scoop rolls out of pan and serve warm.

Gwen Stefani Hollabaklava

BAKLAVA

SERVING SIZE
Serves 15 to 20

INGREDIENTS

Baklava

2 cups walnuts, finely ground

1 cup hazelnuts, finely ground

1½ tablespoons ground cinnamon

¼ teaspoon salt

16 ounces packaged frozen phyllo dough (twenty 14-inch x 18-inch sheets), thawed

1 cup unsalted butter, melted (2 sticks)

1. Preheat oven to 325°F and grease a 10-inch x 15-inch glass baking dish with butter or non-stick spray.

2. **FOR THE BAKLAVA:** In a medium mixing bowl, mix together walnuts, hazelnuts, cinnamon, and salt until evenly combined and set aside. Nuts should be slightly larger than crumbs; a few larger pieces are okay.

3. Cut thawed phyllo sheets in half to fit the baking dish.

4. Place one thin sheet of phyllo dough onto the baking dish and brush completely with melted butter. Top with second sheet of phyllo dough and brush with melted butter. Repeat until there are 10 sheets of buttered phyllo dough. Butter the top sheet and spread a heaping ½ cup of walnut mixture onto phyllo dough.

5. Repeat layering with 4 more sheets of buttered phyllo dough and top with another ½ cup of the walnut mixture. Repeat to make 3 more layers of 4 buttered sheets, with a heaping ½ cup of walnut mixture between each layer.

continued →

TRADITIONAL DESSERTS

201

Syrup
⅔ cup water
⅔ cup honey
½ cup granulated sugar
1½ tablespoons lemon juice
About 20 whole star anise, optional

6   Top with a final layer of 10 sheets of buttered phyllo dough. Butter the topmost sheet with extra butter and push down gently. (The phyllo should be layered as follows: 10 sheets, nut mixture, 4 sheets, nut mixture, 4 sheets, nut mixture, 4 sheets, nut mixture, 4 sheets, nut mixture, 10 sheets.)

7   Cut baklava into 4 rows lengthwise, then cut diagonally 2-inches apart across each widthwise cut to form diamonds. See guide below.

8   Bake baklava for 1 hour, or until golden brown.

9   FOR THE SYRUP: While baklava is baking, whisk together water, honey, sugar, and lemon juice in a medium saucepan. Bring mixture to a boil over medium heat. Reduce heat to medium-low and allow to simmer for 5 minutes undisturbed. Remove from heat and cool to room temperature.

10 When baklava has finished baking, immediately pour syrup over baklava.

11 Allow baklava to cool for about 2 hours to reach room temperature before serving.

12 Top each square with star anise, if desired.

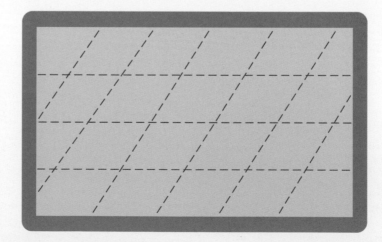

Gwen Stefani

Front woman of No Doubt, Grammy Award winner, designer, philanthropist

"Cause I'm just a girl, little ol' me. Well don't let me out of your sight. Oh, I'm just a girl, all pretty and petite. So don't let me have any rights. Oh, I've had it up to here!"

Dolly
Parton

Most honored female country artist of all time, Grammy Award winner, Academy Award nominee, entrepreneur, philanthropist

===

"Tumble out of bed and stumble to the kitchen. Pour myself a cup of ambition."

Dolly Parton Nine to Five Crock-Pot Peach Cobbler

PEACH COBBLER

SERVING SIZE
Serves 10 to 12

INGREDIENTS

20 ounces frozen peach slices (see Tip) or 2½ cups peeled and sliced peaches (about 5 whole peaches)

1¼ cups brown sugar, divided

3 tablespoons milk (dairy or non-dairy)

¾ cup all-purpose flour

½ cup old-fashioned oats

2 teaspoons baking powder

½ teaspoon baking soda

1 teaspoon ground cinnamon

⅛ teaspoon ground cloves

¼ teaspoon salt

½ cup unsalted butter, divided (1 stick)

1 Lightly grease Crock-Pot with butter or non-stick spray.

2 Toss peaches lightly in ¼ cup of the brown sugar. Combine peaches and milk in the greased Crock-Pot.

3 In a medium mixing bowl, mix together remaining 1 cup brown sugar, flour, oats, baking powder, baking soda, cinnamon, cloves, and salt.

4 With your hands, a fork, or a wooden spoon, work in ¼ cup of the butter until a coarse, crumbly texture is formed.

5 Pour flour mixture evenly on top of the peaches.

6 Cut remaining ¼ cup butter into thin slices and place on top of flour mixture.

7 Lay a paper towel or clean kitchen towel over the top of the CrockPot so that it overhangs the sides and will stay in place once the slow cooker is covered.

continued →

8   Cover and bake for 2 to 3 hours on high or 4 hours on low, or until top is lightly golden all the way across.

9   Serve warm with a scoop of vanilla ice cream, if desired.

If using frozen peaches, remove peaches from freezer and allow to thaw at room temperature for 30 minutes before use.

Mindy Kaling
Kelly Kapooreo
Cheesecake

COOKIES AND CREAM CHEESECAKE

SERVING SIZE
Serves 10 to 12

INGREDIENTS

Crust

2 cups chocolate
sandwich cookie
crumbs (about
25 cookies)

4 tablespoons
butter, melted

1. Preheat oven to 325°F and lightly grease a 10-inch springform pan with butter or non-stick spray..

2. **FOR THE CRUST:** In a large mixing bowl, mix cookie crumbs and melted butter together until all the crumbs are coated.

3. Pour crumbs into springform pan and press crumbs down on the bottom of the pan firmly with your hands or a spatula. Set crust aside.

4. **FOR THE FILLING:** In a large mixing bowl, combine cream cheese and sugar and mix with an electric mixer on medium speed until smooth. Add eggs and vanilla extract and mix until combined.

5. Add sour cream, heavy cream, nonfat dry milk, and flour and mix until combined.

6. In a separate bowl, chop or break chocolate wafers or cookies into small pieces, about ½-inch. Add broken pieces to batter and gently mix with a spatula or wooden spoon until evenly distributed.

continued →

CAKES &
CUPCAKES

Filling

16 ounces cream cheese, softened

⅔ cup granulated sugar

3 eggs

2 teaspoons vanilla extract

½ cup sour cream

¼ cup heavy cream

2 tablespoons nonfat dry milk

1 tablespoon all-purpose flour

½ cup chocolate wafers or thin chocolate sandwich cookies

½ cup semisweet mini chocolate chips (4 ounces)

7   Pour batter over crust, then sprinkle mini chocolate chips evenly over the batter.

8   Place springform pan on a baking sheet and bake for 55 minutes to 1 hour, or until edges are set and center is still slightly wiggly.

9   Allow cheesecake to cool in the pan for about 20 minutes, then cover with plastic wrap and transfer to the refrigerator to chill for at least 2 hours. Remove from pan to serve.

Mindy Kaling

Emmy Award–nominated screenwriter, author, comedian, actor, creator and producer of the first American TV show starring an Indian-American woman

"I will leave you with one last piece of advice, which is: If you've got it, flaunt it. And if you don't got it? Flaunt it. 'Cause what are we even doing here if we're not flaunting it?"

Gloria Estefan

Cuban-American singer and songwriter, Grammy Award winner, front woman of Miami Sound Machine, entrepreneur, Presidential Medal of Freedom awardee

"My mom was a source of strength. She showed me by example that women, regardless of how difficult life may get, can do it all."

Gloria Esteflan

FLAN

SERVING SIZE

Serves 10 to 12

INGREDIENTS

¾ cup granulated sugar

4 eggs

14 ounces sweetened condensed milk

12 ounces evaporated milk

¼ cup whole milk

2 teaspoons vanilla extract

2 teaspoons spiced rum

1 Preheat oven to 350°F and have ready a 2-quart glass baking dish (round or square).

2 In a heavy or nonstick saucepan, melt sugar over low heat until it reaches a smooth, golden brown, liquid consistency. Quickly pour hot sugar into glass baking dish and set aside.

3 In a large mixing bowl, whisk eggs until beaten, about 30 seconds.

4 Add sweetened condensed milk, evaporated milk, whole milk, vanilla extract, and rum and whisk until combined.

5 Pour liquid into baking dish and cover with aluminum foil. Place baking dish into a larger baking pan filled with about 2 inches of water.

6 Place baking pan in the oven and bake for 30 minutes at 350°F. Reduce oven temperature to 300°F and bake for an additional 50 minutes to 1 hour, or until flan is set but center still jiggles slightly.

7 Remove foil and allow flan to cool for 30 minutes at room temperature. Re-cover with aluminum foil and set in the refrigerator for 8 hours or overnight.

8 To unmold, run a knife along the edges of the flan, place a serving plate over the pan, and flip over together. Lift and remove pan.

Lucille Ball

Emmy Award–winning actor, comedian, producer, first woman to run a major television studio, first female inductee into the Television Academy's Hall of Fame, Presidential Medal of Freedom awardee

"I don't know anything about luck. I've never banked on it and I'm afraid of people who do. Luck to me is something else: Hard work—and realizing what is opportunity and what isn't."

I Love LuSeed & Honey Cakes

SEED AND HONEY CAKES

SERVING SIZE
Makes 12 mini cakes

INGREDIENTS

Cakes
1 cup all-purpose flour

¼ cup almond flour or meal

½ teaspoon baking powder

¼ teaspoon ground cloves

3 tablespoons unsalted butter, softened

½ cup whole milk

½ cup honey

1 egg

½ teaspoon vanilla extract

¼ cup pumpkin or sunflower seeds

Topping
¼ cup honey

2 tablespoons pumpkin or sunflower seeds

1. Preheat oven to 350°F and grease a 12-well cupcake tin.

2. **FOR THE CAKES:** In a large mixing bowl, whisk together all-purpose flour, almond flour, baking powder, and ground cloves.

3. Add butter and mix with an electric mixer on medium speed until roughly combined; the mixture will still be quite crumbly at this point.

4. In a medium mixing bowl, whisk together milk, honey, egg, and vanilla extract. Pour the liquid mixture into the flour mixture and mix with an electric mixer on medium speed until combined.

5. Add seeds and fold into batter with a spatula or wooden spoon until evenly distributed.

6. Pour the batter into cupcake tins until each well is about two-thirds full. Bake for 10 minutes.

7. **FOR THE TOPPING:** Remove cakes from the oven and top each with about 1 teaspoon of honey. Sprinkle a few seeds on each.

8. Return to oven and bake for an additional 5 to 8 minutes, or until a toothpick comes out clean when inserted.

Madonna

Musician with over 300 million records sold, Grammy Award-winning songwriter, actor, Rock and Roll Hall of Fame inductee, LGBTQ+ rights activist

"I'm tough, ambitious, and I know exactly what I want. If that makes me a bitch, OK."

Madonna Queen of Pop Tarts

STRAWBERRY TOASTER PASTRIES

SERVING SIZE

Makes 9 toaster pastries

INGREDIENTS

Pastry

1 ⅔ cups all-purpose flour

⅓ cup whole wheat flour

1½ tablespoons sugar

1 teaspoon salt

1 cup unsalted butter, cubed (2 sticks)

2 eggs, divided

1½ tablespoons heavy cream

Filling

1 cup strawberry jam or preserves

1½ tablespoons cornstarch

1½ teaspoons lemon zest

½ teaspoon vanilla extract

1. **FOR THE PASTRY:** In a large mixing bowl, whisk all-purpose flour, whole wheat flour, sugar, and salt together.

2. Cut butter into mixture ¼ cup at a time, incorporating with a fork, a pastry cutter, or your hands until dough is crumbly and clumps together when pressed between fingers.

3. Add 1 egg and the cream and mix with an electric mixer on medium speed until combined, scraping down the sides of the bowl as needed.

4. Divide dough into 2 equal parts and transfer to lightly floured parchment paper. Roll out each piece to a rough rectangle, top with plastic wrap or parchment paper, and refrigerate for at least 30 minutes or up to 8 hours.

5. **FOR THE FILLING:** In a medium saucepan, whisk strawberry jam, cornstarch, lemon zest, and vanilla extract together. Bring mixture to a simmer over medium heat, scraping down the sides and mixing as needed. Allow to simmer for 3 to 5 minutes. Remove from heat and cool.

6. Preheat oven to 350°F and line 2 baking sheets with parchment paper.

7. When dough has cooled, roll each piece into a 9-inch x 12-inch rectangle. Cut one piece into nine 3-inch x 4-inch rectangles and return to the refrigerator. Cut the other piece into nine 3-inch x 4-inch rectangles and transfer to prepared pans.

continued →

215

Glaze

1 cup powdered sugar

1½ tablespoons milk (dairy or non-dairy), plus additional as needed

¼ teaspoon vanilla extract

sprinkles, if desired

8 In a small bowl, whisk the remaining egg. Brush rectangles with egg wash and place 1 heaping spoonful of filling onto the center of each rectangle, avoiding sides. Remove the second batch of dough rectangles from the refrigerator and use to top each pastry.

9 Press down firmly with your fingers on all 4 sides, then seal by pressing down with the tines of a fork across all 4 sides. Brush the top of each pastry with egg wash. With a toothpick or chopstick, pierce 9 holes in each pastry to allow steam to release while baking.

10 Bake 30 to 35 minutes, or until pastry is golden brown. Allow tarts to cool completely before removing from the pan.

11 **FOR THE GLAZE:** While tarts are cooling, sift powdered sugar into a medium mixing bowl. Whisk in milk and vanilla extract by hand or with an electric mixer on medium speed until glaze is thin and spreadable. Add additional milk 1 teaspoon at a time if needed. When tarts have cooled completely, spread glaze across each tart as desired. Add sprinkles on top of glaze, if desired.

12 Tarts can be warmed by heating in a toaster oven or oven at 350°F for 3 to 5 minutes.

When picking a jam to use, look for one with minimal additional ingredients and only natural sources of sugar.

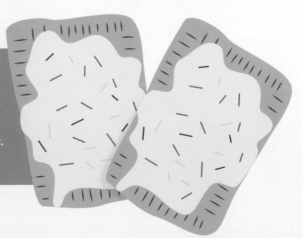

Marshmella Fitzgerald

BROWN SUGAR MARSHMALLOWS

Makes about
2 dozen
marshmallows

INGREDIENTS

¾ ounce unflavored
gelatin
(3 packets)

1 cup cold water,
divided

1 cup granulated
sugar

¼ cup brown sugar

1 cup light corn
syrup

1½ tablespoons
vanilla extract

powdered sugar or
cocoa powder
for dusting

1. Grease a 9-inch x 13-inch baking dish.

2. Gently whisk gelatin and ½ cup cold water together in bowl large enough to hold all the ingredients.

3. In a separate, deep saucepan, combine the remaining ½ cup cold water, the granulated sugar, brown sugar, and corn syrup and stir over low heat for about 1 minute.

4. Raise the heat to medium-high and allow the mixture to reach a rolling boil. Let cook undisturbed until sugar reaches 240°F on a candy thermometer. This will take between 5 to 7 minutes at a rolling boil. Do not become intimidated by the intensity of the boiling sugar; the water in the mixture will keep it from burning.

5. Remove from the heat and slowly whisk the hot sugar mixture into the gelatin with an electric mixer on low speed. Once all of the sugar is incorporated, adjust mixer speed to the highest setting. The mixture will begin to bubble and will change from dark brown to off-white as it comes together.

6. Continue to whisk at full speed until mixture is stiff and fluffy, 7 to 10 minutes. Add in vanilla extract and mix for 1 more minute.

continued →

217

7   Immediately pour the mixture into the greased baking dish and spread as evenly as possible with a greased spatula or greased hands. Do this quickly, as the mixture will harden fast.

8   Allow marshmallows to sit for at least 6 hours or up to 24 hours before cutting with a greased knife or greased cookie cutters.

9   Toss in powdered sugar or cocoa powder to coat.

To make marshmallows last, store in an airtight container between sheets of parchment or wax paper for up to 2 weeks. If marshmallows stick together, dust with additional powdered sugar or a combination of powdered sugar and cornstarch.

Ella Fitzgerald

Dubbed the queen of jazz, Grammy Award- winning singer, Grammy Lifetime Achievement Award winner, Presidential Medal of Freedom awardee

"Just don't give up trying to do what you really want to do. Where there is love and inspiration, I don't think you can go wrong."

Oprah Winfrey

Talk show host, media executive, actor, producer, Presidential Medal of Freedom awardee, philanthropist

"Create the highest, grandest vision possible for your life, because you become what you believe."

Oprahline Brownies

PRALINE BROWNIES

SERVING SIZE

Makes 1 dozen individual or 2 dozen mini brownies

INGREDIENTS

Pralines

¼ cup granulated sugar

¼ cup brown sugar

¼ cup heavy cream

1 tablespoon unsalted butter

⅓ cup chopped pecans

Brownies

1 cup all-purpose flour

1½ tablespoons cocoa powder

½ teaspoon salt

¾ cup semisweet chocolate squares (6 ounces)

½ cup unsalted butter, softened (1 stick)

¾ cup granulated sugar

3 eggs

1 teaspoon vanilla extract

1. Preheat oven to 375°F. Line a baking sheet with parchment paper and grease a 12-well cupcake tin or 24-well mini cupcake tin.

2. FOR THE PRALINES: In a medium saucepan over medium heat, whisk together granulated sugar, brown sugar, and heavy cream. Continue to whisk constantly but do not scrape down sides. Bring to a boil and allow to remain at a boil for about 3 minutes while continually stirring.

3. Add butter and pecans and continue to whisk, not scraping down the sides, until the mixture comes back to a boil; allow to remain at a boil for 1 minute more.

4. Remove from heat and allow to cool, stirring constantly, for about 5 minutes. The mixture will lose some of its sheen and become cloudy in appearance.

5. Pour praline mixture onto parchment paper and spread evenly. Allow to set for at least 10 minutes.

6. FOR THE BROWNIES: While pralines are cooling, in a medium mixing bowl, whisk together flour, cocoa powder, and salt. Set aside.

7. In a larger microwave-safe bowl, heat chocolate and butter together in the microwave in 30-second intervals, stirring between each interval, until completely melted.

continued →

BROWNIES & BARS

8   Mix in sugar by hand with a wooden spoon or with an electric mixer on low speed until combined, then add eggs one at a time, mixing until combined after each addition. Mix in vanilla extract until combined.

9   Add flour mixture about ⅓ cup at a time, mixing by hand or on low speed after each addition until the batter is smooth and no lumps remain.

10 Using about half the batter, fill greased muffin wells with brownie batter until about one-third full and spread evenly with a greased spoon or your fingers. Break apart the pralines and add a teaspoon to the center of each well, avoiding the sides. Top each well with additional brownie batter until just about full. Spread the batter evenly across.

11 Bake for 15 to 18 minutes for full size or 10 to 12 for mini, or until tops are set. Allow brownies to cool in the tin before flipping the tin over onto a long plate or pan to remove them.

This praline recipe will not make a typical praline or "pecan candy," the decadent treat perfected in New Orleans. To make pralines, you will need to add more sugar and less cream, and heat the mixture to 240°F.

Missy Elliott Shoopa Doopa Fly Pie

SHOO FLY PIE

SERVING SIZE
Serves 8 to 10

INGREDIENTS

1 premade pie crust, or 1 recipe Pieris Apfel Crust (page 163)

1 cup all-purpose flour

¼ cup whole wheat flour

½ cup dark brown sugar

½ teaspoon ground cinnamon

¼ teaspoon ground ginger

⅛ teaspoon salt

6 tablespoons unsalted butter, cubed

¾ cup water

½ teaspoon baking soda

¾ cup unsulphured molasses

1 egg

1. Preheat oven to 350°F and grease a 9-inch pie pan.

2. Roll pie crust into a 10-inch circle. Lay prepared crust in the pie pan, allowing edges to overhang by ½ inch; style edges to your liking using a fork or a spoon, or by pinching dough together with your thumb and index finger.

3. Poke holes in the bottom of the crust, lay parchment paper over the crust, and fill with dried beans or weights; this will stop the pie crust from rising or bubbling during baking.

4. Bake pie crust for about 15 minutes, or until dough is set. The dough should be soft to the touch but not sticky, with golden edges. When crust is baked, remove parchment and weights and increase oven temperature to 375°F.

5. In a large mixing bowl, whisk together all-purpose flour, whole wheat flour, brown sugar, cinnamon, ginger, and salt.

6. Cut in cubed butter and work in with a fork or your hands until the mixture is crumbly in texture and forms small balls when pressed together between fingers. Set aside.

continued →

PIES TARTS & COBBLERS

7 In a medium saucepan, bring water to a boil. Mix in baking soda until completely dissolved. Remove from heat and whisk in molasses. Allow mixture to cool for 3 to 4 minutes.

8 Add egg and whisk until combined.

9 Pour half of the liquid mixture into the partially baked pie crust. Top with half of the flour mixture. Layer on second half of the liquid, then top with last half of the flour mixture.

10 Place pie pan on a baking sheet and bake for 35 minutes, or until filling has puffed up and is set.

Missy "Misdemeanor" Elliott

First female rapper to go platinum six times, Grammy Award winner, producer, philanthropist

---

"My style can't be duplicated or recycled. This chick is a sick individual."

Reese Witherspoon

Academy Award–winning actor, Emmy Award– winning producer, author, entrepreneur

"I was warned that on the crazy chance Pacific Standard would acquire any good scripts we would never make it past our first few years in business because there just wasn't a market for buying female-driven material. But like Elle Woods, I do not like to be underestimated."

Reese Witherspoon Legally Blondies

WHITE CHOCOLATE BLONDIES WITH SPRINKLES

SERVING SIZE

Makes 12 to 18 blondies

INGREDIENTS

1¼ cups all-purpose flour

½ teaspoon salt

¾ cup granulated sugar

½ cup butter, melted (1 stick)

1 egg

1 teaspoon vanilla extract

¾ cup white chocolate chips (6 ounces)

¼ cup pink sprinkles

1   Preheat oven to 350°F and line a 9-inch x 9-inch baking pan with parchment paper.

2   In a medium mixing bowl, whisk flour and salt together and set aside.

3   In a large mixing bowl, mix sugar and butter together with an electric mixer on medium speed until fluffy, about 3 minutes.

4   Add egg and vanilla extract and mix until combined.

5   Slowly add flour mixture and mix on medium speed until combined.

6   Fold in white chocolate chips and sprinkles and mix gently with a wooden spoon or spatula until evenly combined.

7   Pour batter into the lined pan and spread evenly with a spatula.

8   Bake for 50 minutes to 1 hour, or until the middle is firm and set.

9   Allow blondies to cool completely in pan before cutting into squares.

BROWNIES & BARS

227

Cher

Grammy Award–winning singer, Academy Award and Emmy Award–winning actor, LGBTQ+ rights activist, philanthropist

"Mother told me a couple of years ago, 'Sweetheart, settle down and marry a rich man.' I said, 'Mom, I am a rich man.'"

Shoop Shoop Cher-y Pie

CHERRY PIE

SERVING SIZE

Serves 8 to 10

INGREDIENTS

4 cups tart cherries, pitted (fresh or frozen and thawed)

1 cup granulated sugar, plus additional for sprinkling

¼ cup cornstarch

1½ teaspoons vanilla extract

1 teaspoon almond extract

2 premade pie crusts or 1 recipe Pieris Apfel Crust (page 163)

1 egg, beaten

1. In a large mixing bowl, combine cherries with sugar, cornstarch, vanilla extract, and almond extract. Cover with foil and set in the refrigerator for 1 hour.

2. Preheat oven to 425°F and grease a 9-inch pie pan.

3. Roll pie crust into a 10-inch circle. Lay prepared crust in the pie pan, allowing edges to overhang by ½ inch; style edges to your liking using a fork or a spoon, or by pinching dough together with your thumb and index finger.

4. Remove cherry mixture from refrigerator and mix well with a wooden spoon or spatula. Pour cherry filling into pie and top with second pie crust. Press along the edges with a fork or thumbs to seal. Cut five 2-inch slits around the center of the pie in a star shape.

5. Brush pie crust with egg. Sprinkle sugar across top of the pie.

6. Place pie pan on a baking sheet and bake for 15 minutes at 425°F, then reduce the oven temperature to 375°F and bake for an additional 45 to 50 minutes until top is golden brown and cherry filling is bubbling.

7. Remove pie and place on a cooling rack. Allow pie to cool for at least 1 hour before serving to allow filling to set.

If using frozen cherries, remove cherries from freezer 30 minutes before using to allow them to thaw adequately.

Whoopi
Goldberg

First African American entertainer to win an Emmy, Grammy, Oscar, and Tony award, talk show host, comedian, Disney Legend

"We're born with success. It is only others who point out our failures, and what they attribute to us as failure."

Whoopi Pie Goldberg

CHOCOLATE WHOOPIE PIES

SERVING SIZE

Makes about 1 dozen whoopie pies

INGREDIENTS

Whoopi Cakes

1¾ cups all-purpose flour

¾ cup cocoa powder

1½ teaspoons baking soda

½ teaspoon baking powder

½ teaspoon salt

1 cup granulated sugar

½ cup unsalted butter, softened (1 stick)

1½ teaspoons vanilla extract

1 egg

1 cup whole milk

Frosting

1 cup powdered sugar

1½ cups marshmallow crème

½ cup unsalted butter, softened (1 stick)

¼ teaspoon vanilla extract

1 teaspoon milk (dairy or non-dairy), as needed

1. Preheat oven to 350°F and line 2 to 3 baking sheets with parchment paper.

2. **FOR THE WHOOPIE CAKES:** In a medium mixing bowl, whisk together flour, cocoa powder, baking soda, baking powder, and salt. Set aside.

3. In a large mixing bowl, mix sugar, butter, and vanilla extract with a electric mixer on medium speed until creamed. Add egg and mix on medium speed until combined.

4. Alternate between adding milk and flour mixture, mixing on medium-low speed until combined after each addition.

5. With an ice cream scoop, drop 2-tablespoon-size portions of dough onto baking sheets. Keep at least 2 inches between each cake, as they will spread. Bake for 12 to 15 minutes, or until set.

6. Allow to cool completely on the baking sheet.

7. **FOR THE FROSTING:** While cakes are cooling, whisk together powdered sugar, marshmallow crème, butter, and vanilla extract. Add milk and whisk until frosting is thick but spreadable . Add additional milk, 1 teaspoon at a time, if needed.

8. Top half of the cakes with a heaping tablespoon of frosting. Top frosted cakes with unfrosted cakes and allow cookies to set on a cooling rack if needed.

These whoopie pies are very large, about the diameter of a grapefruit. For smaller pies, use a 1-tablespoon scoop for the dough and reduce baking time to 10 minutes.

Barbra Streisand

Grammy Award–winning singer, Academy Award–winning actor, Peabody awardee, Library of Congress Living Legend, Presidential Medal of Freedom awardee

"I am simple, complex, generous, selfish, unattractive, beautiful, lazy, and driven."

Rhubarbra Streisand Pie

RHUBARB PIE

INGREDIENTS

2 premade pie crusts or 1 recipe Pieris Apfel Crust (page 163)

4 cups chopped rhubarb (½-inch to 1-inch pieces)

1 teaspoon vanilla extract

1 cup granulated sugar, plus additional for sprinkling

¼ cup brown sugar

⅓ cup all-purpose flour

¼ cup cornstarch

1 teaspoon ground cinnamon

1 tablespoon unsalted butter

1 egg, beaten

1. Preheat oven to 350°F and grease a 9-inch pie pan.

2. Roll pie crust into a 10-inch circle. Lay prepared crust in the pie pan, allowing edges to overhang by ½ inch; style edges to your liking using a fork or a spoon, or by pinching dough together with your thumb and index finger.

3. Poke holes in the bottom of the crust, lay parchment paper over the bottom of the crust, and fill with dried beans or weights; this will stop the pie crust from rising or bubbling during baking.

4. Bake the pie crust for about 15 minutes, or until dough is set. The dough should be soft to the touch but not sticky, with golden edges. When crust is baked, remove parchment and weights, place pie pan on a baking sheet, and increase the oven temperature to 400°F.

5. Toss chopped rhubarb in a medium mixing bowl with vanilla extract. Set aside.

6. In a large mixing bowl, whisk together granulated sugar, brown sugar, flour, cornstarch, and cinnamon until evenly combined.

7. Toss half of the sugar mixture with the rhubarb. Pour the rhubarb mixture into the pie crust. Top the rhubarb with the remaining half of the sugar-and-flour mixture.

8. Cut butter into thin slices and place over topping.

continued →

PIES
TARTS &
COBBLERS

233

9   Top the pie with the second crust and make 5 slits around the center in a star shape. Press along the edges with a fork or thumbs to seal. Brush beaten egg onto pie crust and sprinkle with granulated sugar.

10 Bake for 15 minutes at 400°F, then reduce temperature to 350°F and cook for an additional 30 to 35 minutes, or until crust is golden brown.

11 Remove pie and place on a cooling rack. Allow pie to cool for at least 1 hour before serving to allow filling to set.

Burn your bras, not your cakes.

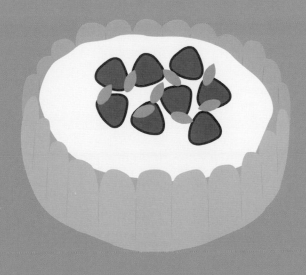

INDEX

ABOUT THE AUTHORS

Karen Cuneo and Grace Cuneo Lineman are sisters who grew up surrounded by smart, fierce woman. Karen, a food scientist, has a particular passion for creating sweet treats, and Grace, a business manager, has a particular passion for tasting these creations. Karen resides in Philadelphia and manages a food blog where she regularly posts new recipes, all of which are pre-approved by Grace. Grace resides on the other side of the Betsy Ross Bridge, in South Jersey, with her growing family.

ACKNOWLEDGMENTS

Turner Publishing-Allison Murray-Marcy Cuneo-Emily Cuneo Desmedt-Dave and Ellie Cuneo-Ashley Landgraf-Julie Lineman-Maggie Fallon-Jennifer Kelley-Jayne Zurek-Roxanne Schmid-Laurie Hooke-Danielle Reinhard-Katie Thompson-Peggy Rust-Casey Adams-Angelica Ross-Adair McCafferty-Melissa Chin-Andrea Dean-Sonia Barnabas-Mary Ellen Cuneo-Jackie Furdyna-Cattie Sherlock-Lauren Beals-Kelly Lineman-Edith Bobb-Debbie Bobb-Danielle Sowers-Lindsay Forbes-David Cuneo-Kevin Lineman-Richie Hooke-Kevin Desmedt-Marguerite Desmedt-Louisa Desmedt-Zuzu Desmedt-Samuel Lineman